MY LIFE AS A BOWL OF CHANGES

Roya Parsay

authorHOUSE

AuthorHouse™
1663 Liberty Drive
Bloomington, IN 47403
www.authorhouse.com
Phone: 833-262-8899

Published by AuthorHouse 10/19/2020

ISBN: 978-1-6655-0257-3 (sc)
ISBN: 978-1-6655-0256-6 (e)

Library of Congress Control Number: 2020919084

Print information available on the last page.

Any people depicted in stock imagery provided by Getty Images are models,
and such images are being used for illustrative purposes only.
Certain stock imagery © Getty Images.

This book is printed on acid-free paper.

I dedicate this book to, Babak, my one and only son.

CONTENTS

Preface ix

Chapter 1   The names whispered in our ears 1

Chapter 2   1952–1953 4

Chapter 3   1953–1958 6

Chapter 4   My maternal grandparents' house 10

Chapter 5   My teenage years, 1960–1969 14

Chapter 6   Going to America, 1969 18

Chapter 7   Earlham College, 1969–1970 23

Chapter 8   Back to Iran 27

Chapter 9   1972 29

Chapter 10   Second summer vacation and back to Iran, 1972 32

Chapter 11   Back to Purdue, 1972–1973: Meeting Bahman 34

Chapter 12   Meeting my future in-laws 38

Chapter 13   Visiting the seaside 42

Chapter 14   An accident, a new car, and travels 46

Chapter 15   1974 49

Chapter 16   Returning to Iran, end of 1974 68

Chapter 17   Getting our own one bedroom apartment, 1976–1977 72

Chapter 18   Getting pregnant, 1976 75

Chapter 19   Returning home from the hospital after giving birth, 1977 80

Chapter 20   Plans made behind my back, 1979 83

Chapter 21   Living with my sister, grandma, and mother, 1979–1981 87

Chapter 22   Taken advantage of in Berlin, 1980 89

Chapter 23   The day in May: My aunt's arrest and execution, 1980 94

Chapter 24   Period, pregnancy, childbirth, breastfeeding..................................99

Chapter 25   My mother and father....................................100

Chapter 26   My former mother- and father-in-law....................................106

Chapter 27   My paternal grandparents 110

Chapter 28   Iran-Iraq War, 1980–1988 114

Chapter 29   Leaving Iran for Switzerland, 1981....................................116

Chapter 30   Seeing my child again in Switzerland, 1981–1983 137

Chapter 31   My mother in captivity over a visa, 1983....................................141

Chapter 32   Rescuing one person from the war, 1983....................................145

Chapter 33   A surprise house guest....................................150

Chapter 34   Babak's visitations, 1984 on after 152

Chapter 35   So-called visitation with my son....................................157

Chapter 36   Life goes on 160

Chapter 37   Babak moved to America and his graduation 163

Chapter 38   During separations from my child 166

Chapter 39   Death of Grandma Zinat Joon, 1992 168

Chapter 40   Mother's breast and, later, bladder cancer, 1993–2001 170

Chapter 41   Jobs I held in my life: Little odd jobs between jobs, 1974–2016...181

Chapter 42   Living in Reston, 2003–2005: A woman and the challenges
              in her life 187

Chapter 43   My political life, 1994–1998 191

Chapter 44   My publication, 2000 200

Chapter 45   Monterey, 2006 215

Chapter 46   Other events in Monterey, 2007–2017 218

Chapter 47   Babak's wedding, 2008....................................221

Chapter 48   Self-respect and happiness....................................224

Chapter 49   A Letter to My Son....................................227

Chapter 50   Quotations....................................229

Chronology of Events....................................232

PREFACE

The contents of *My Life as a Bowl of Changes* are just my memories and the stories of one person's life. The book describes the days of my life with my family and the people I met along this journey. Please don't generalize that these stories apply to an entire country or religion. This is the tale of one out of millions, and in no shape or form do I want to put down or raise up any nationality or religion. I am what I am, and this is my unedited life.

If your life has been full of mistakes like mine, then writing about it would be, as it has been for me, kind of torturous. But at the same time, doing so has clarified a lot for me and for others.

Only the mother remembers how a child is born and the feelings during the days she carried the child inside her. The child has no memories of those months that he or she is able to recollect. So the mother always remembers, and the child needs to be reminded. The child can only witness the birth of his or her child but can never recollect the birth of him or herself. Memories are made throughout the years that a child is raised, and I did not have that opportunity as other mothers did. So one of the focuses of this book is describing the days of my life with that point in mind.

The second point of focus is women's equality. I'm not addressing the topic in the sense of saying that everything a man does a woman should be able to do in order to get equality. Rather, I'm speaking to our differences, along with the fact that some things a woman does—childbirth, breastfeeding, periods, and so forth—are impossible for a man. A consideration of those differences in workforce laws and the rules of society is what's missing now, and I fight for women's equality in that sense always.

In the best seller, *Educated*, Tara Westover explained that all the events she was describing had not been approved by one of her brothers and were totally approved by the other. A psychologist said, "We all see the events with our own camera adjusted to our own brain and attitudes and feelings." No wonder the author of *Educated* had to change the name of one of her brothers so that she would not be sued. But in the end, she shared her story publicly and loved it. The same is happening here. I am telling the story from my perspective—sharing what I witnessed and got out of the events described in *My Life as a Bowl of Changes*. Whoever disagrees with my depiction can write his or her own book. Also, I did not change people's names but sometimes just said a person's first name. So here we go. I will describe my life as a bowl of changes or, in other words, share the unedited days of my life.

At times, it may seem to you that I am repeating an event, but parallel to each event in one's life, many other events are happening. The start of one event could be the end of another that had started years and years ago. So each event should be explained from different angles each time—like in the series *Midsomer Murders*. So when I talk about my mother and her death, simultaneous with my divorce and the weird acts of my last husband, I will return to this time from different angles. I was focusing on my mother's death, while my then husband was focusing on other stuff—like leaving for Iran forever. His family knew. I did not. We will get to that way later in this book.

Also if you feel you get lost when it comes to order of events or mixed up on dates, please refer to the chronology of events at the end of the book. Here we go.

CHAPTER 1

THE NAMES WHISPERED IN OUR EARS

I wonder why I never asked my grandparents who their grandparents really were. I had the historians right in front of me and never asked the vital question. To think I could've had firsthand information and narrative, but we mostly shared junk stories, like Prince This-and-That going after the beautiful So-and-So to marry her or the dragons flying with flames coming out of their mouths.

Another thing that I wonder is why most of the Jews in Iran would never reveal their identity. How many Jews did we have in our family? And how much of my blood, though I was born a Muslim, is Jewish? I really do wonder. It seems that, even when we do think of these vital questions, our grandparents are already too old—suffering the beginning of cognitive impairment and speaking with difficulty.

I had the chance to ask those questions when I was in the fourth grade, since I lived with my maternal grandparents. The only information I got was that my grandfather was first a prosecutor, accusing people, and then became a lawyer, defending people. This is the most serious conversation I had with him, other than the time I told him that I wanted to say my prayers in Farsi, our spoken language, as opposed to Arabic, the recommended one. He said it was okay, as long as I said my prayers regularly. From my maternal grandma's side, I heard that her father had such a fine singing voice that the court gave him the title Saidozakerin, meaning "having a good melody."

As for my paternal grandparents, I have no knowledge of who their parents were, let alone their grandparents. I know my paternal grandma was called Batul, but her name was changed to Fakhr Afagh, a very difficult name for us to say. I remember we used to complain to my grandpa half-jokingly about why he had chosen such a difficult name for her, since when we had a sore throat, we could not pronounce her name! I guess at this point you are asking why my grandpa gave her that name. It was because they lived at a time when having a last name was not common. So when they were given the opportunity to have both a personal name and a last name, he chose the last name Parsay (pronounced /Pars eye/ like *goodbye*). It means "coming from Pars," which was the original name of Iran or Persia. I know his original last name was Naraghi.

Their lives as a young couple were all over the newspapers, since my grandma was a pioneer in fighting for the equality of men and women—especially equal education for men and women—which caused them much trouble. I can get to that part later, but did I ever sit down and ask, Who are you? What are your beliefs? Who are your grandparents? No, I never asked those important questions, and how I do regret it.

In the world's eyes, my grandfather was very liberal and advanced. But to me, he was cruel because he did not like my cat—or any cats, for that matter. He poisoned all the cats in the block, mine included. Maloos, my cat, had long hair and lots of fur but was not a pure Persian cat. She was buried in a wasteland adjacent to our house in Darros, Tehran, and my brothers and I cried over her death. My grandpa would also give candy to my cousins, who lived next door and were the children of his daughter Farrokhrou but not to us. The only times he would give us something was on Charshanbeh Souri, a day in Iran like the Fourth of July, and the last Tuesday night before the Persian New Year, on the first day of spring, called Norooz. Children would get a kind of fireworks that we rotated in our hands. For the New Year, we would each get a lottery ticket, and that was it. He was stingy, in contrast to my other grandpa, who was kind and generous. But what did he go through in life? I never knew. He had blue eyes, a tall thin body, and big lips. He drank alcohol made of cherries, even though he was still called a Muslim.

My other grandpa was religious and did not drink alcohol—but he would smoke opium. It was a common practice for older people to have permission from the government to use it, like the easy marijuana available now. I don't approve of either, but to each his own. He and especially his brother looked a lot like Einstein. Their last name was Massih-nia, meaning "Messiah was their grandparents." So voilà, I guess I just found the grandparents of my maternal grandpa.

Now I look at my grandchildren and wonder whether they or even my son will ever ask me these kinds of questions. Maybe I will volunteer to tell them, but I don't think they will have the time to sit down and listen or even care until they are my age. Maybe this book will be the answer to all these questions and beyond.

My first memory in life is the birth of my second brother, Farhad. He shares his name with the hero of a narrative poem by the Iranian poet Nezami. The poem says Farhad loved Shirin, and also the king Khosro Parviz loved Shirin. But mainly I think my parents chose the name because it rhymed with the name of my other brother, Farzad. I still don't know why parents give their children names that rhyme with each other's or names all starting with the same letter of the alphabet—as if all their lives people will notice that they are connected.

Anyway, my younger brother was born in Tehran, and I remember in the hospital I peeked through the basket and saw an ugly creature like a frog and wondered why everyone was oohing and aahing at him. I was four years older than him and two years older than my other brother, Farzad, whose name means "born from glory," which was the meaning of my mother's name, Shokouh. His real name, however, is Mosaddegh, after the political figure, much admired by my father, who liberated the oil of Iran from foreign hands. My sister Shahla ("beautiful eyes") was three years older than me, and I was called Roya ("dream"). I remember my maternal grandpa saying some prayers into my newborn brother's ears and saying that his name that was whispered in his ears was Ali. This was a custom I have never understood. Why have one name but another name whispered in one's ears? I never asked whether I had another name too.

CHAPTER 2

1952–1953

I was born on November 6, 1952, fifteen days late and with my nails and hair already grown. That's how stubborn my mother was. Giving birth to a second child, she knew how much it would hurt, and she put it off as long as possible. The city of my birth was Abadan on the Persian Gulf, when my father was on a six-month mission there as a judge from Tehran. For some reason, in Iran they called prosecutors serving as judge *ghazi*, which is also a word for a special sandwich rolled up with bread and cheese. As a child, I wondered why every morning we ate my father's job! Children do pay attention to any little detail, and I can see that in my grandchildren now.

Abadan was a very warm city and had most of Iran's oil. At the time, Mosaddegh was popular in Iran, and my father was pro- Mosaddegh, while my mother was pro-Shah. That was not the only difference my parents had with each other. Nor was it the only thing they argued about. Rather, it's one example of a thousand differences between them. Still, they fell in love with each other. My father, only twenty years old and studying law when they met, wrote a series of poems for my mother. If you attached the beginning and end of each line of verse and the beginning of the second line of the poem, each would spell my mother's name, Shokouh Aghdas Massihnia. However, until the day she died, my mother thought that only the beginning of each line spelled her name. She hated her middle name Aghdas, not knowing her daughter—me—would marry a Baha'i later. Their holy book is called Aghdas (or Aqdas). Life has many surprises.

In 1953, my family moved back to Tehran. I was only six months old when a day came that changed my life. My paternal grandpa, whom we called Agha Joon, decided to play a game of repeatedly tossing me into the air and catching me. My mother has told me that I cried in pain. I had an aunt who was a physician, Dr. Farrokh Rou Parsay, and later, she was the first woman to serve as secretary of education in Iran under the Shah. She diagnosed a blockage or twisted intestine caused by the rough play.

I was rushed to the hospital for an emergency operation. In 1953, this was a very risky procedure. Cutting through my small tummy left a large scar that I still bear today. To me it looks like a snake. The surgeon, Dr. Morshed, told my mother, "If she passes gas, then she is saved."

Mother stood by my side all night. When I expelled, she ran through the hospital corridors shouting, "Good news! She did fart! She did!"

That was the start of my anal fixation, as I learned years and years later. After that, I was considered disabled, as if made of china and easily broken. My protective mother would not let other children play with me, as she worried they might kick or hurt my belly.

Later in school, I was exempt from regular exercises with the other students. This exclusion weighed heavily upon me. To escape, I took up swimming and bicycle riding, which were deemed safe for me.

CHAPTER 3

1953–1958

We lived in the southern part of Tehran on Jaleh Street. One day, Mother returned with a large bandage on her face. I was so scared I ran away. I found out later that she'd had a nose job. I don't know why—she really was as beautiful as she appeared to me and had a nice body.

When I was five, the servant, herself only a young girl, took me to the Jaleh movie theater. The theater caught fire, and the servant left me and ran away. I was under the feet of all the people running out. All I saw were shoes and stockings. I started to pinch people's feet, but all the escaping crowd did was to make their steps longer so as not to kick me. No one stopped to help me.

At last when the crowd had cleared the theater, a policeman came to take me out. He saw the servant crying and asked her, "Does this child belong to you?"

"Yes, I am the servant."

"Where do you live?"

"In the next alley."

"Okay," he said, "follow me."

The policeman knocked at our door, and I remember my father quickly grabbed me. He listened to the policeman and whispered to me, "Don't worry. You can have a bottle of milk all to yourself tonight." I then forgot my pain . It was typical at this time that a bottle of milk was left on top of my two brother's beds each night. I did love milk so much that sometimes I would take their milk. Even though I had my very own bottle waiting on top of my bed that night, I kept wondering why no one had stopped to pick me up. Why did everybody hate me? Why did no one rescue me? What was wrong with me?

It took years to learn the collective behavior of people in crises.

I also remember that once I had a severe case of diarrhea, sitting on my potty in the room. My father shouted, "I want to sleep, and it smells so bad! Take her somewhere else!"

My mother took me outside to the yard. We were both shivering, and she was swearing at my father. I felt so guilty, believing I was the cause of their quarrel. I was so affected I developed the anal fixation that I still have to this day. Parents' words and actions strongly affect children.

I wish I had been taught how to have a sweet tongue and not to be so harsh and straightforward. I was taught by mother that, if you don't say all you feel and think and also if you are hiding something, then you are guilty of some issues. If you have a clear conscious, you will not hesitate to say the truth and all you feel. A diary was not a private matter under my mother's surveillance.

Sometimes she would say a girl should be like a camel with a long neck, meaning it should take a while for a word to pass through your long throat and reach your tongue. Did I ever practice that? No! Did I get the punishment for the consequences? Yes! Did I stop? No. Why not? The message in my brain said, if you hide your thoughts and feeling then you are guilty of something. Even more strongly, it told me, don't ever lie. My brain liked and accepted that message. Now these days on Facebook, for security reasons, I lie about where I live. However, if I feel you are unjust to me, I will tell you so bluntly. Believe me, I am trying to be more in control every day. I'm listening to CDs and DVDs and reading books about psychology as much as I can.

So that being said, you can guess that I don't have many close friends. And my family and son hate me for that. But believe me. I love my son. And the last thing on my mind is hurting him. However, I can only take a limited amount of wrong judgments about me. Maybe this book will help to explain.

I looked at some pictures in my album, and the first one I saw was of my mother holding me before her nose job. In the photo, I am six to eight months old. So it could have been taken after my first operation and before my second operation. I look good and chubby. I was told my parents put a sign on my dress that said, "Please don't kiss me." I believe they did the same to my sister and brothers, afraid of germs, something my son and his family are concerned about too.

My son tells me not to visit his family without giving notice. I am also not to come if I have a cold. And I am not to use perfume either.

In the next picture, we all are around my mother. All the children are sitting down. I am trying to imitate my sister, holding my hands under my chin. Another picture shows me and my mother next to a river in Damavand, a city close to Tehran with famous mountains. I have my hair weaved, by her I think. I remember all the people were shouting and running away, saying there was a volcano—that Mount Damavand had erupted.

That is the extent of my early childhood memories. I do recall from my later childhood being ready to start school. And I remember the schools that I attended were called Behesht, Golshan, Mehr Taban, and Kasaee.

In the county of Darros, north of Tehran, we lived right next to my aunt and her children, and we all would go to Behesht. That was the first school I attended. I also remember the doorman would call, "Shirin, Sokhan, Parsay, all come to the door." (He was calling our last names, and sometimes all the children thought they should come to the door too!) He was announcing who should come to the door because his or her ride or parents were there. A lot of trust was given to him, although he was not a security man or a police officer. We just had simple trust .We always all got home safe and sound. My memory of Behesht was that the principal was a kind gentleman. Also I do remember once two teachers played naughty and drank and even had an affair in an empty classroom at lunchtime, and he fired both of them.

Once my cousin Kambiz who was very talented in the English language, was our substitute teacher for English hour. On that class, I got 19 out of 20, and he gave me some papers to correct. I threw them back at him and said, "We don't correct others' papers if we don't get 20."

He was looking at me as if to say, *Hello. I am your teacher now, not your cousin. Listen to me.*

But I did not, stubborn as I was.

He also was my private English tutor for a short while. One of the composition titles he gave me was " If I Were on the Moon." I was puzzled why "I" came with the plural "were." I said I didn't know what to write. He said "You always talk about I and me, me, me. Why can't you do that here?"

I liked him and his brain.

We had jokes about him and how angry he was the time the servant broke his statute of a rooster. "Let me know when the maid comes back," he said.

The next day, he was woken up to be told that the maid was here. While we were afraid that some blood might be shed, he just scratched his head and said, "Naneh, did you break my rooster? But why did you break my rooster?" and immediately went back to bed. We all laughed at that story for a while as an inside joke, imitating Kambiz.

At one point when he was a bachelor, he lived in the upstairs section of our house with his classic records and taught me English. The last time that I saw Kambiz, he was visiting my mother and we all heard on the radio that the Prime minister was executed. Prime Minister Hoveyda was killed by firing squad after Iran's 1979 revolution—sad but true. We will get to those days later in this book. While I was writing this book, I heard Kambiz's daughter, Kathy, a beautiful dentist, died in her sleep. Life's games are unlimited.

CHAPTER 4

MY MATERNAL GRANDPARENTS' HOUSE

Here I would like to tell you about my maternal grandparents' house in Kharabat on Tir Street in downtown Tehran. I lived there for two years and went to an elementary school called Kasai. You could see the sign announcing "Dr. Farhang Massihnia" on the right side of the house next to the door. The proud moment that my grandma put that sign outside her house was the best day of her life. My uncle—tall, with blue eyes, and just returning from Germany—was loved by all. He was the best and kindest heart doctor I ever had. He lived upstairs in that house. He constantly read books on his specialty as a heart doctor.

When you entered the house, you had to pass a long hallway to get to the yard and the house. There is no picture of that house. How I wish there was. It was the oldest house ever. The basement and first floor were original, and the second floor was remodeled. Anyway, when you got to the yard, you saw a small *baghcheh*, a little garden with two tall maple trees and a small shallow blue pool with a fountain in the middle. A bit further along were jasmine plants with white flowers and the best aroma in big pots next to a greenhouse. Then came the steps to the first floor. To the left of these steps were steps that led down to the basement and kitchen.

At the end of the yard was the bathroom. This was the only bathroom for the whole house, and it was outside. We had to go there summer and winter. It did not bother anybody, especially me with my bathroom issues, because I was away from everybody and outside. How much more privacy can you ask for? Persians have this habit of washing themselves every time they go to the bathroom. What is called a bidet here is in the form of a tool shaped like a watering container called *aftabeh*.

Every house in Iran has an aftabeh or two. Washing your private parts is a must after any activity done in the bathroom. As a Muslim or an Iranian, this was a custom obeyed by all. To this day, I have one in my American house, and all my Iranian relatives and friends do too. We can't live without an aftabeh.

Anyway, after going up those steps, you would get to another long passage called *eyvan*. You would enter the house, and immediately, you would see the samovar, always boiling with fresh tea in a teapot on top of it. Someone was always in that area. Either someone was using the samovar or someone was in a little servants' room under the stairs behind the samovar that led to the second floor. The servants were like relatives and part of the family. They had three servants—a mother and two daughters. The mother was called Khaleh Shokat, and the daughters were Mehri and Zari. The original servant was a nanny to my mother and uncle. She was Khaleh Shokat's mother and was called Naneh. She was with my grandparents family from Kermanshah, a province of Iran's neighboring Iraq and where my mother was born. She came back to Tehran with the family and raised my mother and my uncle Farhang. She had a bad temper, I was told, but was loved by all like a favorite nanny.

I had my second operation for a hernia and my appendix and to repair the first operation there while attending to Kasai Elementary School, across the street from my grandma's house.

I returned to my grandma's house from the hospital after my second operation and went back to my school across the street. I still had bandages on my belly, and all the students in my class hugged me and welcomed me. Each hug was painful, but I was glad to be among friends. I have to confess that, since my family actually lived uptown, I looked at them as different but loved them.

Still, I write of many places and people, such as my best friend Mitra. Or from Kasaaee School, I remember Homa Baghee, Ostovar, and Kotob. We called each other by our last names. I remember Kotob was a white half-blond girl. She said that, when they cooked halva for the last religious ceremony, they saw the hand of Imam Hossain on it the next morning—another superstition (*khorafat*). We were kids of ten years old and knew nothing but to imitate the grown-ups.

So I was back eating delicious food and sitting next to grandpa while he smoked his opium. I also ironed my ribbon that was part of my school uniform with the steam coming from a samovar.

More of my maternal grandparents' story

I had the sweetest maternal grandparents. I lived with them for some years, and those were the best and most peaceful years of my life. My grandparents, called Zinat Yamotahari and Mehdi Massihnia, were in love and peaceful harmony with each other. If I had not had them, I would have thought that most parents were cold to each other or fought, having my parents and paternal grandparents as models. My grandpa's last name meant that Messiah was his grandparent. His brother Hossain looked just like Einstein. My grandpa, called Agha Joon, was the kindest man I ever saw—though, like all of us children, I never knew him when he was young. We knew he had another wife before my grandma and had a son with her. His name was Mostafa, and we sometimes would see him visiting my grandpa.

My uncle once told me that my grandpa was drinking and playing cards—or, as he put it *long mibast*, which literally meant he would wrap a special cloth around his waist and go and play dice for money. I never knew that until I was forty years old and having a conversation with my uncle Houshang. Oh, the stuff you don't know until you ask and dig into matters.

My maternal grandparents had four children—my mother, Shokouh Aghdas and then Daee (Uncle)Houshang, Daee Farhang, and Daee Bijan. My grandpa was smoking opium at around sixty years old when I knew him. He did not drink or gamble. He wouldn't even watch TV from the corner of his eyes, thinking he might see naked women on TV. He prayed daily and would encourage me to pray too, even in Farsi and with no hijab. At their house, I would pray like a normal Muslim, with a long head cover and in Arabic. He really loved me maybe because I lived with them. I also know that, on his deathbed in the hospital due to enlargement of his heart, he would tell all the nurses that he had the prettiest and sweetest grandchild and they should wait to see me when I came to visit him.

Unfortunately, taking me to the hospital was in my sister's hand, as she was three years older than me and could take me there. I was not old enough to be allowed to go to the hospital by myself. My grandma was living with us for that period. Once, upon returning from school, I asked my sister to please take me to see Agha Joon. She said no. I never forgot her refusal and have never forgiven her.

The next day as we were waking up, my aunt and her husband walked in and told my mother and grandma that my grandpa had died. I must have been in the last year of school, and he was only sixty-three. My grandma curled into a fetal position and then put her head on the ground and cried. I could feel her with all my heart.

They did not take to the burial ceremony, and he was buried in a holy place called *shabdolazim*. I remember walking around the house, crying and asking God, Why? Why? That was the first death in my life that I could feel—the first time I really knew the person who had died. It hurt me to the core, considering my feelings were on my sleeves. My nerves were wired very close to my skin, and I would always be more sensitive than my siblings. Agha Joon was my father and friend. He was always kind—unlike my other grandpa.

I decided then that I would always take care of my grandma—the kind of promise a child makes to herself. I tried to make sure, in my own limited way, that my grandma was happy and gave extra attention to her. She liked me too. At times, my mother was jealous, wanting to know why I loved my grandma more than her. But grandma was always smiling at me, hugging me, and taking care of me. She always showed her love to me. Mother, on the other hand, was angry. She criticized me, planned my life, and insisted that I had to obey only. Naturally, I liked the sweeter mother figure, thou my mother loved me as much as my grandmother did but could not show it. As the Buddhists says, "She was not skillful enough."

In my maternal grandparents' house, they lived happily, not luxuriously. They had jasmine flowers, pigeons, tea with samovar, and the most delicious food. They prayed and were peaceful. That house was a heaven for me, though it was not at all a luxurious house. That is why I've always felt better and easier around very ordinary people and not people who live plush types of life.

CHAPTER 5

MY TEENAGE YEARS, 1960–1969

When I was a teenager, I started praying in my own way, meaning I didn't wear a hijab while praying and also that I translated the Muslim prayers into Farsi and recited my prayers in Farsi as well. I used to have long hair, and every time I would sit and put my head on the *mohr* as Muslims do, my long hair would be all over the carpet . My parents and siblings and even the servants would pass by and look on and laugh. I was happy and satisfied with that way of praying, and they all preferred either obeying the customs or not doing it at all. I was different all right. My parents, my sister, and one of my brothers never showed any interest in religion, but my youngest brother did. He would even fast. But I never did due to my surgeries during childhood. I think my father was praising Satan for not bowing in front of Adam, a rebellious angel. The devil was brave and a freedom fighter in my father's eyes. My mother perhaps did not believe in God, especially given all the misery she had to deal with and having raised four children and going through three divorces with my father.

I need to explain here that my sister and brothers are all educated. One is an accountant. My brothers have master's degrees, and one is mechanical engineer. But my sister and I are very different.

Living is a form of being unsure—not knowing what comes next or how.

I remember at those ages I was either studying or swimming or playing with my cousins who lived next door. My father's sister, who we called Ammeh Joon, lived next door with her husband, General Shirin Sokhan, and four children. Hamid was the oldest son. Then Nahid was my sister's age. Mahshid was my age. And Navid was closer to my two brothers' age. So we each had a playmate. We had one of the best childhoods and would either swim in our little pool (depth wise) or their bigger and deeper pool. We created many games—from playing shop or newspaper making or café with fake menus to something like jeopardy and chess and other intellectual games. If my parents were not fighting most the time, I could say our childhood was perfect. We would play lay-lay (hopscotch) until they would call us or drag us in. The fact that the alley we lived in off of Sheybaney Avenue in the northern part of Tehran was a dead end meant that we children could play lay-lay or any other game we wanted. The whole alley belonged to us kids.

Once some thieves were robbing the house in front of ours, which belonged to my father's aunt and their sons, and Nahid and I were playing lay-lay. We just watched them take a radio, rugs, and other stuff out of that house and put it in a van at the end of the alley in the street. We thought that they were moving. We just wanted to play. And we did so without disturbance, until the policeman came and asked us about what we'd seen. We couldn't describe anything except that there were two men, but we could have described the stone we were playing lay-lay with in perfect detail.

One day, I was playing and climbed the cherry tree and fell. My feet got some blood on them, and I had to listen to a lecture about how a girl should be careful, since her virginity may be damaged doing too much boyish stuff. My mother's lecture when she would take us to the public bath was, "From being pure to impure is just one step." Or she would say, "If a girl happens to be loose, whether you keep her in a glass or not she will become loose and impure." My sister and I had to listen to that lecture so many times.

But once I was riding a bicycle and I hit the wall. I could feel the seat of the bicycle deep in me and my throat felt funny and was very painful. I was bleeding. My aunt, a physician, was looking at me in a different way, and my parents were whispering. The next day, my father took me to the coroner's office and asked the doctor there to check me. (Since he was a judge, the fastest doctor to be found was the coroner.) That was the first time I had been examined down there—kind of gynecology style.

The doctor said, "It looks okay."

I saw, for the first time, my father worried. He begged the doctor. "Listen, this is too important in her life. Please, please recheck."

I was just lying there and thinking, *Do I have cancer? What is so important?* At the age of no internet, no nude pictures, no nothing, my knowledge was minimum. I thought my father was so advanced in his thinking and so liberal, but when it came to his own daughter, he was like other men. So the doctor examined me again and said it was okay. Up to my wedding night, I was worried about whether or not I was a virgin.

Even when I told my husband that I didn't want to be a virgin on my wedding night, he said, "Let's wait." He was another man, educated abroad and open-minded. But when it hits home, all men are the same. I had some pinkish blood on my wedding night, so I think some of it was damaged by that incident.

When I started going to high school, which was called Reza Shah Kabir High School, my mother chose my friends, where I sit, and everything else. I was totally under her control. My friends had to be A students, and my field of study had to be math. I was seated next to Fati, Guity, and Roya. Roya's father was the head of the navy in Iran, and it was her place I would go to study. In her house, the servants would serve coffee with white gloves. Her father had to leave Iran after the revolution, and their life was ruined—as was true for millions after the revolution in Iran.

Days and nights would pass with our parents fighting. We kids would go to school pretending to have a normal household and studying.

Sarah, 1968

While we were going to high school my cousin Nahid, who was three years older than me, graduated and went to the United States with the American field service. She stayed with an American family called the Linders. After she returned, the Linder's daughter, Sarah, who was the same age as Nahid, came to Iran and stayed with Nahid's family. Since we were neighbors and were together from morning till night, I was there when Sarah opened her suitcase. She had brought lots and lots of tampons. She thought Iran had no tampons or maybe that people rode camels. That was how Americans thought of Iran in 1966, and there was no internet—and no Google Maps either—so they could actually see what the country looked like.

Anyhow, Sarah was a tall, sharp, and beautiful girl, and I practiced my English with her. My brother, Farzad, was a very young teenager of fifteen years old or so, and he loved Sarah. And they call it puppy love.

It would turn out that I would stay with the Linder family on my first visit to the United States. They lived in Iowa City. My parents trusted them, and I spent two months in their house before I went to Richmond, where I had another set of American parents called the Millers. I miss them all.

CHAPTER 6
GOING TO AMERICA, 1969

When I first came to the United States, I flew with Iran Air to Frankfurt, Germany, and then to Chicago, and from there to Des Moines, Iowa. I was wearing a dress that had two big pockets. But inside my dress, my money had ben sewn in behind the pockets by my mother. I only had my passport in my little purse and the tickets.

Up through Frankfurt, everything was okay. I was studying my little booklet with some words and their meanings and also memorizing a sentence that my father wrote in English for me, "I am sorry, but our customs are different." That was the answer I was supposed to give to any boy who would ask me out. I had to say no and this sentence.

As soon as I got on the plane from New York to Chicago, something happened that made me panic. Suddenly, the pilot was on the loudspeaker saying something. This was a real American speaking English, and I understood nothing. What happened to all my high school studies of English? What had he said? Was it important? I looked at the other passengers and saw no panic on their faces. I asked the person next to me, "Excuse me, what did he say?"

He said something, and I did not understand him either. There went all my self-confidence—all the A grades I had gotten in school. My heart was beating rapidly. I hoped the pilot would not announce anything important.

We got to Chicago, and I had to change planes to go to Iowa. My American parents, Sarah's parents, lived in Iowa City. I got lost in the huge airport of Chicago. It was four times bigger than the airport in Tehran. I was almost crying, and I asked a woman for help. She gave me to a flight attendant, and we ran like hell to get to the gate. When I walked onto the plane, all passengers were looking at me as if they were quite angry. I had caused a ten-minute delay. I crept into my seat and tried not to look at anyone.

At last, the announcement came, and I heard Des Moines. I hurriedly started to apply some makeup—powder on my face, mascara, and lipstick. In Tehran, a capital city, many people wear makeup, and this was especially true during the Shah of Iran's time, when there was no mandatory hijab. But I noticed that, in Iowa, people seldom had makeup on at that time, and I looked quite out of place. My American parents, Mr. and Mrs. Linder, were waiting for me, and as soon as I saw them, I regretted putting so much makeup on. Here I was, a seventeen-year-old wearing lipstick and mascara, and my American mother had no makeup and no special hairdo or special dress on. She was plain and simple. I guess that was the last time I put so much makeup on for a long time.

We got in the car, and the Linders knew how little English one understands when just having arrived from a non-English-speaking country for the first time. They spoke slowly and in short sentences. I saw cornfield after cornfield and even an orange snake crossing the highway. There was no heavy traffic—as opposed to Tehran, which was full of cars and constant horn blowing. We got to Iowa City, 120 N. Dodge Street. I knew the address by heart, since my cousin Nahid had lived here, and then Sarah was in Tehran. We'd mailed her letters and that address had been a constant mention in our household. Somehow, Iowa was interwoven with my destiny. Even my roommate in college, now a lawyer, lives in Des Moines. Becky is her name. I'll get to that later.

We got to their house, and it looked nice from the outside. It was an old, beautiful three-story house. They took me upstairs and showed me a beautiful room with a bed and two chests of drawers and said, "Roya, this is your room."

As soon as they left me to unpack, I kissed the ground. I was free of my parent's fights and my mother's constant controlling. And on top of it all, I had my own beautiful room. Thank God and thank America.

The next day, I woke up not remembering where I was. Why were the sounds of the streets different? Where were the mountains surrounding our house? And gradually I figured I was in the United States of America. The only two Americans I had known before coming to the United were Sarah, the AFS exchange student who had lived next door to us in my cousin's house, and Dr. Lawrence Strong, the chemistry teacher in Earlham who we'd met in Iran. I could not wait to see both. I did see Sarah soon, but to see Dr. Strong, I had to wait to get to Richmond, Indiana, on the border of Ohio and Indiana, where I would attend Earlham College, a private Quaker college. That seemed so far away now, although it was only some months away.

My American mother suggested I take a summer course at an Iowa City high school. The first day she walked with me and showed me the way. I was looking at all these boys and girls sitting together and talking. In Iran, my grandparents would say, "Putting young girls and boys beside each other is like putting fire and cotton next to each other." So always they were making sure we girls and boys didn't get close to each other. Here in this school, boys with long hair relaxed and sat on the stairs in front of the high school. And I was very cautious not to get near them—so I wouldn't burn!

After a few days, I was told to walk to school alone. I did get lost, but I found my way. On the way back, I passed a movie theater, and I said to myself, *Why not see a movie?* I looked at the name of the show, and it said *Valley of the Dolls* . With my poor English and seeing the word *dolls*, I thought it might be a children's movie, like *Sound of Music.*

I entered the movie theater, and only a few people were there. It was the middle of the day, and the movie got weirder and weirder. By the time it was finished, I was so ashamed I ran out of the theater. I never told my American mother that I saw that movie. It was a shock for me. I learned to be cautious, since freedom meant bad or good were available, and choice was very important. In Iran, there would have been someone at the door who would not let me in to see porn movies or those kinds of movies. I was adjusting and having culture shock.

First so-called date

One day, I came home and my American mother, Mrs. Linder, told me that a boy in our class had called and asked me out. He was a guy from Ethiopia. I always liked black boys after the movie star called Sydney Poitier. But since we had almost no Africans or African Americans in Iran at that time, I am ashamed to say that, in my eyes, they all looked alike—until I stayed longer in the United and learned to distinguish them. The only black guy I had seen in Tehran was this soldier standing at the American embassy's entrance as a guard. I loved him and would look at him for a long time. I wanted to marry him—a teenager daydreaming.

At any rate, this high school kid came and took me to a movie and bought me some popcorn. I thought he was cheap buying me popcorn, but my American mother said, "It means that he likes you." But all the time, I was reciting in my head, *Our culture is different*—my father's famous sentence engraved in my notebook and in my brain.

The guy never asked me out again, since I guess he thought, *What do I do with a girl who can't speak English and is not into kissing either?*

I met some Iranians called the Abadis, and met an American girl in my class who took me horseback riding. Plus, my cousin Hamid came to visit me from West Lafayette, Indiana. Then after a month, my aunt and General Shirin Sokhan, her husband, came to visit the Linders and me. It was so good to see them. I was trying to be brave, and I was so lonely and wanted to speak Farsi. At that time, my aunt, Dr. Parsay, was the secretary of education in Iran and the first woman elected in the Shah's cabinet. She was studying US schools to bring ideas to Iran and the education department.

I also went on a trip with Sarah, my American sister, and her boyfriend to Milwaukee, Wisconsin. I loved the cheese and chocolate. Sarah's boyfriend had asthma. I hadn't known anyone in Tehran who had that disease, as my circle of friends was limited to high school girlfriends and relatives. I became very scared because Sarah said that sometimes he couldn't breath at night. I liked both Sarah and her boyfriend. I also learned what kohlrabi was. My American mother planted it in her yard, and I loved that vegetable from then on.

One very embarrassing moment for me was the time that my American mother and I went to a pizza place, and she asked me to wrap the leftovers so we could take them home. OMG, I was looking around making sure no one would see me doing that. In Tehran, no one ever took whatever was left on his or her plate home. It was not at all customary. I was humiliated. But the next day I was hungry, and the leftover package was in the fridge. I began to like this new custom.

Time went by too quickly that summer, and soon I had to go to Richmond, Indiana, and start my school. I did not know that another culture shock was awaiting me at Earlham College.

CHAPTER 7

EARLHAM COLLEGE, 1969–1970

At last, September came, and I went to Richmond, Indiana. I can't remember whether I took the Greyhound bus or flew to Indianapolis and then took the bus to Earlham College. I entered a little town where the only person I knew at that time was Professor Larry Strong. I never called him Larry because we never called our professors or teachers by their first names. But that was another culture shock—that it was acceptable to call anyone by his or her first name, especially the president of a college. I did not know at that time that the town hated us because Earlham was such a liberal college. I loved it at the time. I saw many people with long hair, peace signs and jeans. I myself wore jeans and had long hair for the whole year.

Just last week, March 2020, after fifty years, I went to an Earlham reunion at the Pelican Grill close to Newport Beach, California—mind you, with people ten years older or younger than me—and I felt like I was eighteen again. I loved it.

When I started at Earlham, I went to visit the foreign student advisor, and he assigned me a roommate. Her name was Becky. She also had long hair; hers was reddish. Becky's father had a farm in Iowa, and her mother was a golf pro and very nice. Her brother served in the Vietnam War and came back with psychological problems. Who wouldn't? Now I know that the poor soldiers aren't treated well when they return and have a thorough psychological evaluation.

Becky's real name was Rebecca. (I never understood why, in the United States, Rebecca is Becky, Richard is Dick, William is Bill, and John is Jack. I still don't.) She had a great record player that she put between our beds. I hung all my Persian belongings—a samovar, beads, handmade bags, and stuff on the wall—and she did not mind. My bedspread was from Iran, among my items of Persian culture. I just did not have any Persian music records. But Earlham once invited Khatereh Parvaneh, a female singer from Iran. That was how advanced the culture was in that little private Quaker college.

I was given a job as a salad girl in the cafeteria to help me financially. I met some American Baha'is. They were all nice, not knowing that, in my future, the Baha'is would play a big role. There were no Persians in the college except me, so my English improved quickly—very quickly. I was even dreaming in English.

Among my courses, one was field hockey for a physical education credit. One day as I was playing, I saw a little house next to the field containing only one large room. I asked, "What is that?"

I was told, "The meeting room."

So I thought it was a room that the professors met in. (Remember, there was no internet or Google then to research anything, and my English was poor.) Then I asked my roommate, "How come there is no Quaker church around?"

And she said, "That's it, the meeting room."

So I looked on the bulletin boards to see when they met. I wondered why there was no cross or Star of David or a moon and star on the building. Inside, there was nothing but a rectangular room with benches and chairs circled around it. I had a list of questions in my hand to ask the priest. Some people walked in and all sat down, and I waited for a priest to start the ceremony. All were quiet and sat there with their eyes open. I thought, *This is a thinking room.*

After a while, one by one, they all got up and left. It just happened that, on that day, no one had anything to say, and I was left with my list of questions in my hand, still waiting for a master of ceremony or Quaker priest to show up.

I was told later that the Quakers gathered, and, if someone had an inspiration, he or she would talk. It was so simple, so nice. When I told this story at the reunion, I saw the current president of Earlham, Anne Houtman, was laughing so hard. She was a Quaker .

I did meet Dr. Strong and took a course in chemistry with him. My major was chemistry, but it became my minor after a year. I loved it that Dr. Strong was working and researching on water—a solution that is solvable in the majority of chemistry compounds, which is a wonder in itself.

Meeting Jeff

I also, for the first time in my life, had a date with a grown-up boy but never kissed him. We held hands only and enjoyed each other's company. His name was Jeff Hatchette. He was a student and a baseball player. I had no idea what baseball was. He somehow understood my culture and—guess what—he was half black and half American Indian. I really liked him. We went to a school dance together, and he brought me flowers.

Our special relationship ended when I left Earlham. Another mistake? Who knows how life takes us and changes our decisions, attitudes, and relationships. I still like him for the little knowledge I have of him. But life never brought us together again, and it took me further and further away from him. When I went to the Earlham reunion this year, 2020, I wished to see him there. Graduates from all different years were there but not him. Maybe he doesn't live around California, maybe he isn't even in the United States. I just know he was a very good baseball player—a sport that doesn't exist in Iran. I couldn't figure it out, but I would attend his games. I wish him well wherever he is now, hopefully with his wife and grandkids.

As I am writing these lines, the American classic movies program on TV is showing the movie *Love Story*. That was the movie Becky and I went to see, as it was made and shown that year. But our main reason for going to that movie was that another Earlham girl who was more experienced than Becky and I had seen the movie. Knowing that both Becky and I were virgins and had never even kissed a boy, she'd told us that there was a scene that showed a French kiss. Well, at that time, they would not show too much of love scenes—not even the same couple in a bed making love. At any rate, I remember that we both saw that scene and said (not knowing how it feels), "Yuck. Is that how it's done? His tongue was in her mouth and vice versa. So gross." In another coincidence, I am watching this movie again now with a totally different perspective.

I made a huge mistake longing for Persians, instead of learning more of the new culture I was in—American. I started looking for Iranians. I asked around if there were Persians in town. I found one gentleman, who was married to an American. Also, a professor told me there were some Iranians in town who were related to the king. I was surprised and found out they were related to the Zand dynasty, an old dynasty in Iran. I located Parin and Tye, her sister, and became friends with them. There was also Behi, their other sister. Nooshi . All the sisters were married to Americans, and their mother, Mrs. Mohandes Zand, was there too. The mother, a very strict person, brought the four sisters to America. She was pro-Mosaddegh, a nationalist figure who helped Iranians claim the ownership of their oil from England. They told me that Tye was delivered by Mosaddegh's son, a gynecologist, and that her mother hid Mosaddegh's and/or Dr. Fatemi's car under leaves and green beans in their house. Taraneh (Tye) became like a sister and mother to me. But many years later, when she refused to be a witness in my last divorce court, that friendship was damaged.

I also found Rooja, my high school classmate, at Ball State University and she came to visit me. She and I went to Purdue to visit my cousin Hamid and met a lot of Persians at Purdue. So I applied for a scholarship for Purdue, and I got it. My English got worse, and my knowledge of American culture diminished, since Purdue had a larger number of Iranians who I was soon in constant contact with.

In addition, Purdue University gave me a much better scholarship and gave me credit for some of the math classes I had taken at Tehran's high school, like Calculus 101. I also met this guy called Amir through my cousin Hamid in his house. I saw a picture of a caricature of a girl who they said was his girlfriend, called Maryam. I never thought she would become my-sister-in-law and that we all would live in the same house. Life has its surprises always. Whoever you meet might mean something, only years later. But I am jumping ahead of myself.

CHAPTER 8

BACK TO IRAN

At last summer arrived, and I flew back to Iran. I missed my family too much, especially my grandmother. Again relatives came to the airport and greeted me. I hugged my grandma, and my father pushed me into the car so I wouldn't kiss the others, especially any boy relatives who had come to see me. It's funny he did not know what I had done in the United States, but he was sure I was still a naive girl. And guess what? He was right. I had gone all the way to America and back and had not kissed a boy. I looked just the way I had when I left but with longer hair. For the first time, after a whole year of wearing just jeans, I was wearing a dress again. I did not want to give my family a shock by exiting the plane as the hippie that I had been the whole year. The only exception was that I did not smoke any marijuana, since I was allergic to it, but my ideas and dress and hair were all hippieish.

While in Iran I felt that I had changed some, I was starting to be double cultured. I was careful about some stuff and carefree about others. Once my sister took me to the handicraft store of Iran to buy some Persian stuff to take back to America with me. She asked me, "Do you like this?"

I answered, "I think so," which was a straight translation of the reply in English. She got angry and said, "What is to think about? Do you like it or not ?"

My siblings made fun of me no longer knowing the latest songs. And when I would say, "I checked my mailbox," they would laugh at me. In Iran, people don't have mailboxes like they do in the United States. Mail is delivered by hand to the resident or the servants. It is not safe to have mailboxes that are accessible by all.

I also spend most of the summer at a seaside camp called Ordoo. I again felt somehow different from the others. My double cultural beliefs were kicking in. I was happy to see them all, and they were happy too but felt that I was getting even weirder than I had been when I'd left. Remember that I was different from them to begin with, and now that was even more so.

At last the time came to return to America. But this time, I returned to West Lafayette, Indiana, not Richmond, Indiana. I was entering Purdue University, a much, much bigger and better school than Earlham, with my cousin Hamid and all forty some Iranians who attended Purdue. But Earlham College had better qualities than Purdue University that my young and inexperienced brain could not understand at the time.

Purdue University, 1971–1972

While I was still living in Richmond and right before leaving, I got a call from a friend of my cousin Hamid, who was looking for him. His friend's name was Majid. Whoever Majid introduced me to, I fell in love with. First it was Ghasem, his roommate, and then Bahman, who would become my first husband.

As I was talking to Majid, who was asking about Hamid, his roommate, Ghasem, came to the phone and started talking to me. How does love happen? I had not seen Ghasem yet, but I felt I loved him. I still do, since, when you fall in love, you can't fall out of it. I was only with him—the first boy I'd kissed in my life—for a year. But the memory of that time would always be with me. He would die in the revolution in 1979. Again, I've jumped ahead.

Majid, from day one, became my brother and confidant. To this day, for some odd reason, I think I can trust him to help me. Or maybe I am wrong. But that was the kind of friendship that developed with him.

The first day I went to Purdue, I found the campus way different from that of Earlham. The weather was much colder, and the students all had short haircuts. No signs of any hippies around. It was so cold that, in my chemistry lab class, which was at 7:30 a.m., the guys would walk in with icicles on their beards and mustaches.

CHAPTER 9

1972

I entered Purdue and was assigned to a dorm called Fowler Courts, which housed five girls. The reason I remember the address and name of the dorm is that I still have the Purdue ID card in my possession after so many moves in my life. And after having lost so much in the mail from Switzerland to America, some items survived. My roommate was a pretty little girl who had a boyfriend from her hometown called Joe. The girls made fun of her and her visiting boyfriend because they said you's, instead of you are. They were from a small Southern town.

The other reason the girls did not like my roommate was that she started dating one of the girl's boyfriends, Charlie. One day, as she was getting ready to go on a date with Charlie, I asked her, "Why don't you tell him that you also have a boyfriend called Joe?"

She said, "Why? Then he would not date me anymore!"

Illogical answers are simple too.

My bed was on top of hers, and I was witnessing two different boys coming to our room. One day as I was sitting on my top bed, the whole gang of girls in our dorm came to our house and put whipped cream and toilet paper all around and on the mirror and on her bed. They kept saying, "It has nothing to do with you, just her."

I was so afraid that Joe, who was three times bigger than Charlie, would find out and, in the ensuing quarrel, hurt me too. But Charlie was a student, and Joe was a visitor, so my roommate could arrange their comings and goings well. I did not like that culture in America.

The other girls—to show me they had nothing against me—volunteered to pierce my ears, which had not been pierced up till then. They brought ice and needles and pierced my ears. How you trust anything and anybody at a young age.

Changing dorms, my major, and ideology

But by the end of that year, I decided to change my room and soon moved to the graduate house, which offered one room per person and no roommates. I also changed my major to computer sciences, and chemistry became my minor. Mother agreed, as long as there was a chemistry in there. Computer sciences was a new field, and we used to carry a long box of cards as our program, which was punched by a machine. God forbid if we dropped that box; we had to punch the whole program again.

I was falling in love fast, and the Majid's roommate, Ghasem, was the guy who took my heart away. He was religious and fasting but leftist, as he had fallen in love with Che Guevara and Mao. I liked the little red book of Mao, the Chinese leader at that time, the same as my paternal grandpa, Agha Joon Parsay did, but could not totally commit to him. I could sense that, in the book, every thing looked rosy, but in reality, people were not happy in China. I was part of an Islamic association and would pray there at noon but would stand next to the men and not behind them as was customary. My revolutionary ideas were always with me, especially the women's movement part of it—and they remain with me today.

Anyway, the Confederation of Iranian Students was being formed at that time, and I and my cousins Hamid and Kambiz and Ghasem and Shahla and some others were part of it. Shahla, Ghasem, Bijan, Kambiz, and Hooman became very involved, but me and Hamid and Majid were evaluating. Some, like Reza and Ali, were not involved at all. I remember that Majid had a book of Mosaddegh on one side of his bed and a book of Shah on the other. For Ghasem, there was a book on Mao and Che on one side and one on capitalism on the other. We were a bunch of young people who just wanted to revolt and had no idea how.

Poor Hamid was reading all these ideologies while his mother, Minister of

Education Dr. Farrokh Rou Parsay, was the first woman in the Shah's cabinet; his father, General Ahmad Shirin Sokhan, was a general in the army of the Shah; and most of his friends were against the Shah. Majid thought that Hamid's mother summoned him to Iran when he was in his third year of school so that he would not be absorbed by the revolutionary students. Hamid left a year after I went to Purdue.

I remember all the students would have a meeting every couple of weeks and talk about the situation in Iran, with no cell phones or internet and limited books. We had a bunch of navy students. One of them gave me good tips on driving lessons. I did not have a car or driving lessons. People who had a car were valued above others. Ghasem had a Camaro, Reza had a GM car with loudspeakers in it, Majid bought a secondhand car for $200, and Ali S had a yellow sports car. At that time, I recognized cars by their colors—unless it was one of the cars my father used to have, like an Alfa Romeo or a Chevy.

I was torn apart between these political songs and the music of confederation and Mao. Ghasem bought a huge poster of Che Guevara and hung it in his room. Majid, his roommate, made fun of all groups and was very independent. He was concentrating on studying and making money. Maybe he was the most focused of us all.

Shahla was the most active, and she gathered all these young boys and they all became a changed person. She herself married the head of the confederation group, Amini, later divorced him. And Ghasem died during the revolution in Iran while trying to rescue people from the Shah. Kambiz later became a capitalist and rich. Majid and Reza became rich too by working. Poor Hamid, my cousin, died of heart attack after the new regime in Iran killed his mother by firing squad.

We'll get to that part of the story later. But for now, I am a sophomore at Purdue University and head to toe in love with Ghasem.

CHAPTER 10

SECOND SUMMER VACATION AND BACK TO IRAN, 1972

The summer came, and I returned to Iran. When I got there, I hid a copy of the confederation magazine in my *Hair* music record. I was touched by Mao's ideas and the confederation, but being a religious person, I could not identify with them. When I told my father I had hidden a copy of the Confederation of Iranian Student's newspaper in my music 33d record that I'd brought from America, he got very angry. He said that was a great and unnecessary risk, especially since I did not belong to that group. He said that, if Savak (the secret police during the Shah) had found it, I would be in prison. I was surprised that he himself was so pro-Mosaddegh and such a revolutionary person, but when it came to his own daughter, he was scared. He immediately took that newspaper to show my aunt, who was the secretary of education at that time.

I never saw that paper again. But when, as usual, we went to the seaside camp, my aunt and the prime minster of Iran, Hoveyda, came to visit the camp. In the middle of the program, my aunt called me, and I sat on the floor between her and the prime minister. They were sitting on the steps of the amphitheater.

My aunt said to Hoveyda, "She is the one who brought that paper."

The prime minister said to me, "Really? You did?" And as he spoke, he took the cane he was always carrying and shook it above my head. The gesture was like he was trying to hit me with his cane to punish me, and I held my hands over my head to prevent him.

This picture became the title for *Ayandegan* newspaper. Underneath the picture was written, "The Prime Minister is visiting the discipline camp of Ramsar." For a newspaper title and picture, it was nice. But we become doubly scared—afraid Savak might catch me. But thank God, nothing happened.

Upon my return to Tehran, I asked Hamid to come to a movie with me so I could see Ghasem. The three of us went to a movie, but Hamid sat between me and Ghasem. I figured something was changing in Ghasem. He was no longer coming to visit me, and he referred to me as being from a class not close to "the people." This was not so. Yes, my aunt was the secretary of education, but my family was not rich or anything like that. Mother was a teacher and had become head of the Tehran branch of extracurricular activities, and my father was a prosecutor. So why was Ghasem treating me that way?

Much, much later (like thirty years later), I found out that Majid was pressuring him to make a decision and not leave me hanging—either marry me or leave me. Majid told me that Ghasem would cry and say that he was a changed person and wanted to devote his life to people and politics.

So when we returned to America and all went back to Purdue, Ghasem told me that he was breaking up with me. I cried and cried. I said, Why did I kiss him? I was glad we had not gone further and that I was still a virgin, but my heart was broken badly.

That is when I met Bahman, a Purdue student. And here was that big change in my life.

CHAPTER 11

BACK TO PURDUE, 1972–1973: MEETING BAHMAN

I resided in a dorm called Graduate House. One day, Majid came over and asked me to go to lunch with him. A guy named Bahman was with him.

I said, "I don't want to come to lunch." And I saw Bahman got sad.

I felt sorry for him and I said, "Okay I will."

Bahman then got a happy face. I did not know that Bahman was the one who was interested in me and had asked Majid to arrange a meeting. I think he'd seen me around the campus and in the cafeteria where we all exchanged some chitchat as a group.

At lunch, Bahman seemed different, not so Iranian in behavior but very Persian. He said he had seen me in the cafeteria before. He also told me he had a scholarship from the oil company where his father worked and that he was willing to pass it on to someone who needed it.

I replied, "I already have mine from the head of the oil company, Dr. Eghbal, and I also have one from Purdue University and don't need it."

At that time, the Shah of Iran wanted Iranians to get educated and come back and build the country, so the oil company was assisting the effort. My aunt was minister of education in Iran, and later I found that Bahman's father was minister of defense and very close to the Shah. They had a different religion, called Baha'i. I was a Muslim. I had no problem with that but found out later that some very educated people from my family were very much against it. Anyway, I talked mostly with Majid that day.

Some days later, Majid came back and told us that Bahman had a backgammon set made of gold and ivory, which was common in Iran as "Khatam-kari," but nobody had seen such a backgammon set. A bunch of us Iranian students went to Bahman's apartment. One of the girls, Susan, acted as if she knew Bahman and had been to his house before. I assumed he was dating her and didn't think more of it. Much later, though, I found out this was her first time going there too, but she was acting.

Later I heard Bahman was throwing a party at his house for my birthday. I asked Majid, "Why me? Isn't Susan his girlfriend?"

"No," he told me. "Bahman has a girlfriend called Kerry in Louisville, Kentucky. She is an American."

I said okay.

At the party, everybody except me had feeling of marriage shaping up there.

Bahman got me a toy dog with dots on it, since I had said I would like to raise a Panter or tiger in my house one day. He sent some azalea flowers to my dorm. However, he signed the card on it too quickly, and I thought it was a Bob or Rob who I knew.

He asked me, "Did you get any other presents?"

"Yes," I told him. "I got some azaleas from Rob."

"Who is Rob?" he asked. "That was from me."

I thanked him and thought he was very kind but had a girlfriend. So I forgot about it.

Again I saw him at another Persian party with other students, and his girlfriend was with him. Kerry was from Kentucky. She was a newspaper columnist and very clever but she got breast cancer. I didn't think it was nice of Bahman to leave her at that difficult time. She later had a surgery and lost one or both of her breasts and then another reconstruction operation, getting beautiful breasts. I saw her years later in Baltimore.

One day, Bahman came to my dorm. And while we were in my room having tea, he told me, "Pull up your dress. I want to see the scar on your tummy from the operation." He was referring to the operation I'd had at six months old and again at twelve years old.

I did, and he kissed my scar. I immediately started really liking him and started a deeper friendship with him, as close a relationship as a virgin could have with her boyfriend.

Once Bahman left for Kentucky to see Kerry, and I tried to forget him. I was happy that he made me forget another guy who'd I thought I was in love with. His kindness was much needed by my soul. Bahman also helped me when I had my wisdom teeth removed. He took care of me. He always loved to take care of a sick person (usually that person was his mother). There were the signs, but I had no clue of the psychological term called "love needy "or "love craving person."

He returned from the Kentucky visit, came to take me to a mutual friend's house, and wanted to hold my hand.

"Go back to your American girlfriend," I said and pulled my hand from his.

"Listen to me," he said.

"No," he replied, running ahead of him. We were in a parking lot.

He stopped me and said, "Listen. I want to marry you."

I stopped and said, "What? Really?"

He said, "Yes. I am serious."

Wow, things changed, and I was smiling again.

I remembered a letter my mother had sent me. "Whoever was taking care of you when you had your teeth surgery is a kind man and you should marry him," she had written.

At that time, a decision about a marriage was based on education and kindness and a good family. He had all three.

A short while after that, his mother, Touran Khanum, and his sister Jaleh came to Purdue, and we met for dinner. When I think of how young and naive I was and how I behaved, telling jokes, I cannot stop laughing. I think if my son had brought home a girl like that, I would have laughed too. First, I could not find anything I liked in my closet. I had to wear a cotton mini skirt with dots on it and a short-sleeve blouse. I was shivering the whole time. Those who have been to Purdue University and West Lafayette know how cold it gets. Maybe that dress was the reason that, some years later in Geneva, the same sister, Jaleh, took me to a store and helped me choose some clothes. I am a hippie at heart and never cared about wearing matching color clothes or what-not. At that dinner, I was telling jokes to his mother as if she were my age. Anyway, that passed, and they liked me.

CHAPTER 12

MEETING MY FUTURE IN-LAWS

But Baha'is have a custom that all aunts and family had to approve of the girl before a member could marry her. He planned another surprise meeting when we each went to Iran for our summer vacation. I did not like that. I was an independent, free woman, and I disliked any interference.

He once invited me to his house in Elahieh, Tehran. It was a huge house in a huge garden with a tennis court in it and a huge pool that "we never swam in." But at least they played some tennis on the court. Once the Shah's helicopter passed over and slowed down to look, maybe because of the bright lights on the tennis court.

Anyway, I went there because Bahman had said, "No one is at home."

As we were walking in the garden, I saw four women sitting there, and they were his paternal and maternal aunts. I changed my route and did not pass them. Polite or not, at any moment in my life, my actions were based on women's lib—proving you can't do that to women. If I can't immediately react with that goal in mind at certain moments of my life, I make sure I prove it later.

Another day, he came to pick me up and suddenly said, "I have to pick up my parents."

We went to Dr. Nahavandi's house (he would later become my son's doctor and our family doctor). I saw the doctor and his wife and Bahman's parents all standing outside. Everybody was looking at me as if I was some kind of merchandise. That made me angry. If he would have asked me to meet his parents, just as I had already met his mother, I would have gladly accepted. But this way—no.

I sat in the front seat of the car with Bahman. And his parents, General Sanii and Mrs. Sanii, sat in the backseat. I sat in the car turned halfway toward Bahman and halfway toward his parents—an awkward way to see General Sanii for the first time. He was the minister of defense in the Shah's cabinet; a close friend of the Shah; and, for a short while, minister of agriculture. A long time before that he had been the deputy to Mosaddegh (the main figure who helped to nationalize the oil of Iran) when Mosaddegh was minister of defense. He also was the special guard to the Shah in his youth and sometimes would sleep behind his door. A joke in the family was that a devoted soldier would make his hands and legs as straight as he could while he was asleep so he was respectful to the king even then. I'll talk about him in detail later. It is the culture in Iran that, to respect elders, you never sit with your back to them, so during the whole ride, I was sitting that way.

Well I passed those tests in their eyes, and one day, just his mother and he came to our house to ask for my hand. His mother, Touri Joon as my son calls her, wanted our house to be the place to have the wedding. We had a large house in Darroos and two large baghchehe, little gardens. We decided to have the dinner of the wedding night there, cooked by the officers' club (*bashgahe afsaran*). And Aadel, the family cook, had a hand in making the delicious dinner.

They had three demands. One was that no alcoholic drinks should be served. The second was that the ceremony should not be performed by a mullah with a turban. A relative (Bahram) found a clergyman with no turban, and he even gave him a bottle of whiskey to thank him for officially marrying us. Some registration of marriage offices had clergymen like that too. The third demand was that my mother should continue paying for my last year of university until I graduated. We accepted. The day that my mother presented the travelers checks to pay for my tuition, though, Bahman, out of misguided pride, took them from her and tore them up.

My youngest brother got angry, took Bahman to another room, and told him, "You can treat your wife the way you want to. But you must treat my mother with respect."

I went to a tailor called Mansoor in the Mohseni Square in Tehran for my wedding dress. It was a very simple dress with a green belt and muguet flowers, as little white flowers with green leaves were the theme of my dress. For my hairstyle, they sent me to Ratavoos, Matavoos, two famous Armenian hairdressers who people close to the Shah or court would use. But Bahman's family told me to say it was my birthday so the hairdresser wouldn't charge for a wedding, which was more expensive. My other sister-in-law, Maryam, came with me too. As I gave over the bridal tiara made of Muguet flowers to put on my head, all present in the saloon were quietly laughing as if to say, *Yes, yup it's only a birthday party.*

Also, Timsar Sanii, my father-in-law, said, "Please don't overdo your makeup."

I did my makeup myself on my wedding night. And as they walked into our house for the wedding party, I asked Timsar, "How is it? Do you recognize me?"

He laughed and said, "Yes, khanum" (Yes, ma'am).

In Iran, how and who prepares the bride is a big deal, but I like simplicity and think spending too much money on a wedding is a total waste of money. In the list of our guests were three cabinet ministers, of whom two died by firing squad after the revolution in Iran. Lots of generals and friends and relatives were in attendance, but the most important guest was my maternal grandma. Maman Zinat Joon very bravely came to my wedding, smiled, and loved the whole time.

Some relatives did say, however, "If he is a Baha'i, none of their prayers are accepted by God."

How strange, and they were the educated ones! One of my brothers did not come downstairs to participate, maybe because of the traveler's checks incident.

At ten o'clock, after a nice dinner had been served, the wedding was over. I changed my wedding dress to red pants and a white shirt, and we headed to Hotel Hilton with Bahman's family. At the entrance of the hotel, General Sanii, my father-in-law, got out of the car and gave us a short speech. In his blessings, he said, "Always be respectful of each other and have a happy life."

They left, and we entered the hotel lobby. I started getting nervous, as I was a virgin and did not know what to expect. As the guy was checking us in, I was biting my lips. Because I did not have a wedding dress on, they refused to check us in. Bahman got angry and said, "We just got married. There are flowers sent from the oil company to our room. What are you talking about?"

They wanted a proof of marriage and our birth certificates, which were in the hands of the *akhoond*, or clergyman, who'd married us. So we had to wait until General Sanii got home and call Bahman's parents (remember there were no cell phones then) . The general talked to the hotel manager, and they let us in.

The night that all girls await in anticipation, worries, and fear happened with very little blood, like pink, so it was disappointing. Was it due to my having fallen from the bicycle? The cherry tree? Was this why my father was so worried and had showed me to two doctors, one of whom was the doctor at the coroner's office, since he worked with the justice department as a judge? All for this?

As I puzzled, our room phone rang. Maryam and Amir, my sister-in-law and her husband, who was also a Purdue University student called us from the hotel lobby. They must have been sent by the general to see if all was okay. And they asked us to join them in the lobby. I declined.

CHAPTER 13

VISITING THE SEASIDE

The next day, we headed to my mother's villa at Ramsar, the seaside of Iran, on the Caspian Sea. We really actually consummated our marriage at seaside Ramsar. I learned that so many positions were possible, as Bahman was trying to show me a new world of which I was totally unaware. I remember I was crying after that, and our driver, Deylami, was following my every step at the shore because his boss, Bahman, had asked him to. I needed time to digest married life, and he would not leave me alone. I cried a lot that day, thinking, *Why has the world, in so many ways, evolved around the virginity of a girl? Why so many honor killings in the world? All for a piece of thin skin?*

As I said, everything I did and do has a women's lib angle to it. And from that angle, I was hurt, belittled, and puzzled. I was also hurt that I had asked Bahman to have complete sex before the wedding day, so since he was not a virgin, I would not be one either.

He said, "No. We waited so long. Let's wait one more week."

He was one of the men who respected a virgin more than a woman, and in my eyes, I pitched him in among those who weren't with women's lib.

I disliked that. I returned to the villa later and painted a fish and a bird next to each other—from the depth of a sea to the highest sky.

We returned to Tehran and started living in Bahman's house. It was a small two-story house at a corner of the big garden, where his parents lived upstairs, and we lived in one room downstairs. There were one room and a bathroom downstairs, and two rooms and a bathroom upstairs. The kitchen was still in the main house, which was under construction. The kitchen was used by the servants to cook the food and all. That was how and where Bahman and I started our life together.

After a while, we all moved to the new house. One day, as we were putting stuff around, I saw a picture of an old man in his mother's closet. I said, "Oh. Is that Bahman's grandfather?"

She immediately covered it and angrily said, "No! This is Hazrate Bahaollah" (or maybe it was Hazrate Abdolbaha). That was their prophet, and Baha'i is an advanced religion that have the picture of their prophet but rather not to show the picture of their prophet.

Returning to Purdue

A couple of months after our wedding, I returned to the United States to finish my last year at the University of Purdue. My mother reordered the cashier's checks that Bahman had torn apart, and I headed back to Purdue. Bahman was supposed to follow me some weeks later to start his PhD.

One day, as I was studying, the phone rang, and it was his mother. She said, "Bahman and I are now in England, and he wants me to buy him a Bose loudspeaker. So either I can do that, or I can buy him a ticket to come to America."

That was another big shock I got. *What?* I thought. *He is not just coming to America; he is joining his wife!* I kept quiet. As we were taught to be polite to elders, I just said, "Whatever you wish. It's all up to you." And I hung up.

I was furious. He was a mama's boy to the core. I started disliking him.

At last he arrived with a Bose speaker, and we moved to married students' housing. I loved to watch TV, and he loved his stereo and hated TV. We ended up having the smallest TV on earth, the size of an alarm clock, for me, and the biggest stereo and speakers for him. He never watched TV with me and would even be angry with me if I watched my favorite program. He would argue, "You left me all alone in bed to watch a TV program."

I hated arguing so much, remembering my parents' constant arguments, that I would say, "Okay." I should have said, "How come you don't join me and we watch it together?" Instead I kept quiet for years—until I burst one day.

I also received a letter from his father. Since I kept it, here is the translation:

23 September 1973

Dear Roya,

I have the first letter that I've receive from you, and it makes me hopeful for the future. It is the letter of a girl who is thinking about her future, while I have not yet received a letter from Bahman.

As you have written, in youth, one should get an education to build a better future and also try hard to gain faith and manners. Knowledge and faith are two wings that enable humans to fly to higher goals and humanitarianism, alongside health and happiness proportional to the spiritual values they've gained. Whether in the small environment of a home and family or the vast space of a country or the even vaster world of creation, these wings will give man an opportunity to serve and permission to gain knowledge and proudness.

Dear Roya, Bahman unconsciously has become a follower of you. You have to use this state to secure his health and happiness, which, in reality, is your health and happiness.

I have told Bahman several times to value a spiritual way of life, *manaviat.* Pay attention to the divine providence and don't forget praying and fasting. He should not start a day without attention to God, and no evening should pass without thanking God's infinite features before going to sleep. This is a way that has been glorified, keeping us from corruption and ruin, by religious leaders, and it will guarantee that every unconscious human will reach home.

Dear Roya, Bahman should not waste his time. He should not jump from one branch to the other and become a joker of all trades. He has to gain experience in the same field that he has studied, mechanical engineering. He needs to work during the day and be skillful in his specialty. At nights and evenings, he should register for trainings related to his field or close to that with enduring hardness and difficulty studying, until, if God is willing and it is possible, he gets his PhD. And if this is not done, at least he will be an experienced and knowledgeable mechanical engineer.

He can consult on his affairs at the Iranian embassy with the Honorable Dr. Ordoobadi and the honorable Mr. Amoozegar. And he can also get help from the Honorable Mr. Zahedi, the consulate (Safirkabir).

Now that he is coming to America, try to see that his time is not wasted. He should not be among youth with no manners or those who are too free. He should refrain from drinking alcohol, even one glass of beer and smoking cigarettes, even one cigar. And he should refrain from mingling with people who except trouble, for nothing else is achieved from that.

Wishing your young family a bright future,
General Sanii

CHAPTER 14

AN ACCIDENT, A NEW CAR, AND TRAVELS

Bahman did not start his PhD program because, a short while after he arrived, we got a call from his mother informing us that his father had an accident on the road to the seaside, and the car toppled over. The driver was the infamous Deylami, the guy who was following me step by step at the seaside on my honeymoon. He was immediately discharged. I guess he feel asleep at the wheel. We were told that, by order of the Shah, the general had been taken to the best hospital in New York. Bahman and I flew there. We immediately went to the hospital and saw Touri Joon, very worried and sleeping on a sofa next to the general's bed. We said hello, and Timsar looked and talked normally, which was a relief. He was scheduled to have an angiogram. Bahman accompanied him, and I left to visit my mother.

It just so happened that my mother was in New York too, with some students touring the United States by order of the Iranian Department of Education. My mother took me to Vidal Sassoon for a nice haircut, and we bought some yellow jeans and a top for me. I looked decent again, and we returned to the hotel where Bahman and his parents were.

There, I remember I was sitting in Bahman's lap and acting freely. Now that I am a mother-in-law myself, I do not like to see such scenes, but we were too young and were trying to adopt the American style of life. Bahman had been educated in England. He'd been sent to a pension school in England, maybe Lee School, since third grade and then was sent to America for his higher education. He could not write or read Farsi, but he spoke Farsi.

His parents suggested that he buy a car, and he chose a Porsche—the love of his life. If I'd have let him, he would have brought the car to bed with him. To buy that car, we got some money and had our first American Express card, which had $13,000 or a little more on it for couple of days. We felt rich for those couple of days. Then he bought a Porsche 911 Targa, and we had nothing again.

Every time we felt rich while at school, we would go to a Chinese restaurant in West Lafayette, but we were in New York then.

I also remember that, when I was at school, I wanted to join Bahman in England, so I asked my father to send me $600 "to do my teeth." But I took that money and went to London, stayed with Bahman for three days, and went back to West Lafayette. He headed back to Iran.

Also, I remember that, when we wanted to be anonymous, we flew to California together for Thanksgiving and went to the house of a friend, Sedigheh Salim's, sister, and in walked a guest. It was Janti, Bahman's cousin. You can never hide.

In England, when I flew in with the money my father had sent for my tooth surgery, we stayed at Shahyar Yamini's house. When we spent the night together there while dating, he used a condom, in case something were to happen during our necking session. The next day, I put that condom with his sperm in it in the middle of a street in London. I can't get over what youth do and think.

Years later, we went there with General and Mrs. Sanii. I went to the bathroom without asking where it was, and all thought I'd maybe dated Shahyar once!

Now the Mayo Clinic released the general, and as we were turning the corner from the hospital to the car, he felt dizzy. Timsar had a hard time getting into the Porsche, and Touri Joon and I sat in the back.

Timsar said, "All this money for a small car, and I can feel all bumps on the road?"

He also confessed that he'd faked it at the doctor's office and had managed to get by. We immediately returned, and they wanted to do an operation on his brain. This was paid for by the court of the Shah, and Bahman and I got to stay at the Carlyle Hotel, where Jackie Kennedy used to stay.

The general had his operation successfully. I also tasted my first lobster by Bahman tricking me in that hotel. One day at lunch, Bijan, Bahman's younger brother, who had joined us, ordered a whole lobster. I was staring at the lobster's eyes and refused to taste even a bit of that food. Bijan found it very delicious and was enjoying it, and I was trying to cover its eyes with a napkin. Later on in our hotel room, Bahman ordered a salad and there was some delicious white meat on it. After I ate it and enjoyed it, Bahman told me it was lobster. He tricked me one more time in England, giving me oxtail soup—something I would never have eaten if I had known what it was.

At last, I returned to school to finish my education, and Bahman stayed with his parents. He joined me later, and I got my bachelor's degree from Purdue in computer sciences in 1974.

Bahman decided his father was old and sick and needed him. So I did not continue my education, and he did not go for his PhD. We returned to Iran after my graduation and refused getting a green card, something we regretted later after the revolution in Iran.

CHAPTER 15

1974

The last days at Purdue were mixed with strange feelings, especially since we thought we'd never return to the United States, except perhaps for short trips as visitors. I was feeling at home in the States, but we had to return and serve our country and parents and have children—the traditional goals.

Before departure, I was sitting in our living room with Vahid, a thin and very young boy, who was a student and Majid's younger brother. I asked Bahman to let us drive his Porsche. I don't know why he trusted me and a very young boy to do that. Vahid and I were laughing and having fun, and I was thinking that this demonstrated a lot of trust because Bahman loved his car.

Suddenly, I hit a tree, and Vahid and I stopped laughing. We examined the car. It was okay, but as soon as we returned, I told Bahman, expecting a huge reaction. He ran and looked at the car and saw no damage. Vahid and I took a breath of relief, but that was the last time ever that I was allowed to drive that car—the first and last time.

I saw Vahid some twenty-five years later at Majid's house in Maryland, and he had turned into an old man with white receding hair. I guess I changed too. Sometime after that meeting with him and his wife and children, I heard that Vahid had died of a heart attack. So soon. From Purdue students, I know only that he passed away, along with Ghasem, who was killed during the revolution in Iran. I am not aware if anyone else left us, though some of us from the small community of Iranians studying at Purdue in the '70s know about others. As I was writing these lines, I heard that Mr. Sattari Pour, another Purdue student at my time, died in England, at the end of 2017.

On the way to return to Iran after graduation, 1974

Every student had an allowance to bring a car to Iran without paying duty taxes. Bahman's family wanted to use my allowance and bought a Chevy Blazer. My poor mother, who paid for my studying, accepted it so as to not make my life with my husband difficult. It was totally her right to use this advantage. Anyway, the Blazer was shipped to Iran and was waiting for me to release it from customs as a student returning from abroad, and the Porsche was shipped to Europe. I don't remember how Bahman managed to move his Porsche from the United States to Europe, but we had it when we stayed in London at Maryam's studio.

We flew to England and stopped in London. His mother; his sister Jaleh; and her husband at the time, Mahmoud, were all staying in a studio type of house with a half level as their bedroom. Also there were Maryam and her husband, Amir, who was another Purdue University graduate. I don't know how we managed but I remember that his mother was sleeping on the couch, and Bahman and I and Jaleh and Mahmoud were sleeping on the floor. All of us were young, recently married couples. Maryam and Amir stayed in the half level. My community life with his family started.

I was not happy because I can't go to the bathroom if I'm not alone or in a very familiar place. I never thought I would have to live with others when I met my husband in the United States—and not in a small village in Iran. Now, my son and his wife are not comfortable living with his mother and her mother-in law for a day, but I was going to live in the basement of their house from then on.

I felt so nervous and sad that they called a doctor to see me. She was a Persian psychologist married to an Englishman. We visited them one day and had dinner with them. I remember the doctor's mother, an old simple Persian woman, telling me, "I guess God loves the English more than us. See how much trees and greenery they have, and we don't have that much rain and greenery in Iran."

The doctor diagnosed me as still nervous and gave me some more pills to calm me down.

I said, "I don't see that I fit here and can't love him thoroughly if he is so dependent on his mother and his family."

She calmed me down and advised me to wait and let the pills have their effects.

Well, the plan was that we would drive the Porsche to Geneva, Switzerland, passing through Germany and Austria, and then his mother would join him. I would fly to Iran, and they would drive the Porsche through Turkey to Iran.

His mother and Jaleh and Mahmoud left, and we stayed until the Porsche arrived in England from America. Maryam broke the news that she was pregnant. The next day, she came home and said, "It's strange. Today I put my head on my desk and slept for hours."

We were all young and naive. We said that maybe it was something that came with pregnancy.

In the very early hours of the next day, while Bahman and I were sleeping on the floor downstairs and Maryam and Amir were up in the half level, we woke up with Maryam screaming, "I am dying."

She was in pain, and Amir brought her down and put her on the couch. Bahman gave her some water with concentrated sugar (*nabat*) dissolved in it. Maryam asked me, "Can you check and see if I am bleeding?"

Amir, who was trying hard not to cry, said, "I will do it."

Bahman and Amir called the ambulance. In England, first a social worker and doctor has to come, and then they call the ambulance (a total waste of time). At last, an old doctor arrived after ages and examined Maryam. We heard something like "fallopian tube broke." We knew nothing about that. He called the ambulance. He had to call again and say something like "super emergency." She was bleeding internally, and after ages, the emergency team arrived.

They immediately injected a needle right into her neck, not her arm, and rushed her out. Someone said, "When they do that, it means a lot of blood has been lost already, and they want to be as close to the heart as possible."

As soon as they took Maryam out, I collapsed. I was already suffering some depression, and this was the last straw for me. I woke up with the touch of a person who had some beard but no end to it. I was looking at him for a long time, thinking, *What is this? Why does his beard have no end?* I figured I was in a hospital in England with an Indian doctor (they fold their beards and use a rubber band to hold them).

After the shock was gone, I saw him holding my wrist and looking at his watch. I figured he was a doctor and said they could release me, though I wanted to stay there longer. I knew that, when we would get to Iran, I would have had to live in the basement of Bahman's family's house with all his family and no private kitchen.

We returned, and Maryam was released too. She had lost her first baby. We were young and took it as an event in life.

After a few days, Bahman and I left with the famous Porsche to go to Cornwall and visit his friends before heading to Switzerland. I was relieved because, for two or three days, I had not gone to the bathroom at Maryam's house. I cannot do it if I don't have privacy or if I don't feel safe. Bahman was waiting for me to get severe diarrhea so I would do it anywhere. That never happened because my brain was much stronger. It goes to a childhood event, as a psychologist explained. Anyway, at the first gas station, I was relieved. I was a happy camper again. Don't laugh at me. It is not pleasant, and it's out of my control.

Bahman had ordered a Morgan car in the United States through a catalogue that was supposed to be handmade for him. There, he cancelled the orders, but we saw some Morgans. They were beautiful cars.

The roads to Cornwall were very, very narrow, and hardly one car could pass. It was something like the roads in the *Doc Martin* TV series. At last, we arrived at Flushing, where his friend had a beautiful garden, and it was said that Daphne du Maurier, the famous writer, wrote one of her books there. The next day, there was some noise, as if someone was being murdered. It was coming from the two peacocks his friends had. It was so cold at night. I did not dare move and held Bahman tightly to stay warm

I think we visited Falmouth too. And there we all went to the sea and caught some crabs and lobsters in a basket. Later, they boiled them right there in the kitchen. I saw one walking on the floor of the kitchen. A guy, who was a fisherman, took it and dumped it in boiling water, and I heard the scream. I said, "I will not eat it," and asked, "Why do you eat it that way?"

He said with a heavy accent, "Because they are oogly."

The next day, we returned and went to the ferry boat, to take us from England to France. The rest was just driving. We stayed in Germany to visit my sister and her no-good husband. She was pregnant with her first baby, Sepideh. I stayed with my sister solving crossword puzzles, and Bahman went to show his car to her husband. I never liked her husband, Mehrdad (not to be confused with my last husband with the same name). He looked like a frog that someone had stepped on, and his blue eyes bulged. But my sister was head to toe in love with this creature.

There, I went to East Berlin and saw how one side of the street, from West to East Berlin, changed. Cars on each side of the wall belonged to different times, and how the wall saddened people until President Reagan brought about the demolishing of that wall. I heard stories of people hiding in wheels, how one child was at one side and the other at another. Sometimes help can only come from outside, no matter how much the people want to change something. It was 1974 when I visited Berlin and its wall.

We continued through Austria with its beautiful forests and got to Switzerland and its majestic scenery. In Geneva, we stayed with Jaleh and her new husband, Mahmoud, an international lawyer who has big green eyes. Bahman's mother was there too.

Mahmoud said, "Every time I want to buy cheese for Bahman, I sees which one smells more like socks in a sneaker, and that is the good one for him."

He was a fake guy, and years later, we found out that he was a closeted gay man.

Picture 1 from left to right / top to bottom

- My parents in Abadan near Persin Gulf , she is pregnant with me
- Me & my mother after my operation six month old
- With my mother at Damavand near Tehran
- Two childhood pictures

Picture 2 from left to right / top to bottom

- Family picture Roya, mother (Shokouh), Sister (Shahla), Father (Farrokh pour), Youngest brother (Farhad), Younger brother (Mosadegh, Farzad)
- With sister, Father and me; clothes made by mothe
- With sister, mother and me having matching clothes made by mother

Picture 3 from left to right / top to bottom

- Mother and father while engaged
- Parent's wedding, father (Farrokh pour) is 20, mother (Shokouh) is 16
- With father and my sister, our clothes always made by mother
- My father himself a Judge and a poet with a famous Persian poet Mr. Sarmad

Picture 4 from left to right / top to bottom

- Maternal Grandfather (Mehdi Masihnia) Agha joon
- Maternal Grandma (Zinat Yamotahari) Maman Atish per my son
- Mother holding my uncle Farhang's son, Grandpa (Agha joon), Grandma (Maman zin zin dang dang), Mother (Shokouh), Uncle (Daee Farhang), Uncle (Daee Bijan), Grandma, Maman with hijab, Uncle Houshangs wedding from left to right Mr. Mohafez father of bride, Uncles wife (Pouran joon), Uncle (Daee Houshang), Grandpa (Agha joon Masihnia)

Picture 5 from left to right / top to bottom

- Paternal Grandparents family, Grandpa (Parsay), uncle (amoo Farvardin), aunt (Farokhzaman), aunt (Farokhrou), Granma (Fakhr afagh), Father (Farokh pour), Uncle Farokh Zad is missing
- Copy of the First women newspaper published by paternal Grandma called Jahan Zanan meaning World of Women. They were exiled for publishing that.
- Paternal Family picture, the one in military clothes is uncle (Farrokh Zad)
- Cousin Kambiz, aunt ameh joon, grandpa agha joon, aunt's husband General Shirin Sokhan, Cousin Mahshid, Grandma (mamane bala), Cousin Navid
- Grandpa (Farokh din), aunt (Dr. Parsay) and Grandma (Fakhr Afagh)

Picture 6 from left to right / top to bottom

- Classmates at Reza Shah Kabir High School in Tehran, I am far right
- Same class of high school sitting next to Fatti, Guity , and Roya
- Another day in Reza Shah High School, I am in front with white shirt
- With Purdue University classmates, I am second from right
- Nasi and Guity some high school friends

Picture 7 from left to right / top to bottom

- Leaving Iran for America for the first time with father mother and sister
- Relatives at the Mehrabad airport in Tehran first time going to USA
- With uncle Bijan and Uncle Farhang at the airport 1969
- With Guity, Fatti and Layla some friends same day in airport

Picture 8 from left to right / top to bottom

- In Iowa city with American Parents Mr. and Mrs. Linder
- In the yard of Linders house Iowa city, Iowa
- Showing off how big the bananas are in America

- Swimming at a friend of Linders, Iowa
- In my room that used to be Sarah's room the Linders daughter

Picture 9 from left to right / top to bottom

- With Millers my American parents in Richmond Indiana
- Becky my roommate at Earlham in our room
- Me on my bed at the heart of Earlham dorm
- First date in my life with Jeff a student and baseball player
- With Rooja my schoolmate of Iran in Earlham
- At Tye's house celebratingthe Persian new year March 1970

Picture 10 from left to right / top to bottom

- First time returning to Iran after the one year being away 1970
- Last time in Iran 1992 with friends and family

Picture Eleven 11 from left to right / top to bottom

- Grandma Fakhr Afagh founder of world of women publication 1919 activist in women lib, Dr. Parsay their daughter the first woman as Secretary of Education, Grandpa a journalist and founder of Era of Iron publication.
- Shah of Iran, Prime Minister of Iran, Hoveyda, Ardeshir Zahedi the Ambassador, Mr. Amouzegar future Prime Minister, Mr. Alikhanee Minister of Economics, General Sanii the Minister of Defense
- Paternal Family picture, I am the third one standing from right
- Aunt and mother talking about a project at Caspian Sea for students
- Cousin Mahshid, General Shirin Sokhan, me and Cyrus, Mahshid's husband

شمارهٔ اول (۱۵ دلو ۱۲۹۹) سال اول

جهان زنان

در هر ماه شمسی دونمره منتشر میشود

این مجله فقط راجع بامور زندگانی و لزوم تعلیم زنان نگارش مییابد

مقالاتیکه بامسلک ما موافق باشد باکمال امتنان پذیرفته میشود

قیمت اشتراک داخله

سالیانه (۳۰) ۶ ماهه (۱۸) خارجه سالیانه (۴۰) قران

قیمت یک نمره ۲ قران است

اعلانات سطری ۲ قران

بدون تقاضا وارسال آبونمان برای کسی فرستاده نمیشود

محل اداره: مشهد ـ بازارچه سراب ـ عنوان تلگرافی (مشهد جهان زنان)

مؤسس و نگارنده: فرخ دین پارسا ـ تحت مسئولیت: ف . پ .

مکاتیب باید مستقیماً باسم مؤسس نوشته شود

مشهد مقدس ـ مطبعه طوس

CHAPTER 16

RETURNING TO IRAN, END OF 1974

I flew to Iran and waited for Bahman and his mother to drive the Porsche through Turkey. Meanwhile, I released their Blazer from customs as a student. I looked for a job and found one at IBM as a programmer. Later I bought a Toyota with my salary. Once I went to work with the Blazer, accompanying Timsar, who was going to the oil company every day. On the road, he would sing, and I found out later that he was praying, Baha'i style.

I started my life in the basement of the newly built house of my in-laws in Elahieh. Maryam and Amir lived in two rooms next to the pool. Every day from then on, we all ate together with Timsar and Touri Joon, his parents. Sometime later, Jaleh and Mahmoud joined us, and they lived in the rooms next to the pool. Maryam and Amir moved to the old house, which became a two-story house after some renovations. So now every lunch and dinner was with his parents and Maryam and Amir and Jaleh and Mahmoud. I hated that. I wanted to live independently.

When we'd started our life together, as dowry, I had bought a bed and vanity table. The set was the color of bone and made of leather. The workers took it downstairs, where we lived in two rooms, one bath and no kitchen. The next day, Bahman raised his voice and said he didn't like it and that it should be returned. I was very hurt. It was all I could afford, and every girl takes something as dowry. The workers took it back the next day, and we slept on a simple wooden bed because, as usual, we did whatever Bahman preferred.

My mother kept saying, "Don't argue with your husband and try to have a peaceful life." But I was miserable.

One day, Bahman told me people (meaning his family and sisters and their husbands) didn't like it that you took your shoes off under the table at eating time. The smell bothered them. I said in my heart that I didn't like eating with them and having no kitchen either. Also, I detested the fact that, already, I was under the surveillance of so many people. I wanted to live like a woman of the twentieth century, not a wife of a hundred years ago.

Once I said, "I am going to take a shower," and left the table. His father said, "Tell your wife that it's better if she says I have some errands to do and leave because it's not nice to say that she'll be showering."

Once Bahman had beer at an Armenian friend's house. His parents blamed me.

Starting a new life, 1975

This was how we started our life upon our return to Tehran. I looked for a job, and with my bachelor's degree from Purdue in computer sciences, I could land a job at the IBM branch in Tehran. I was a programmer. I also bought a Toyota with my salary. Bahman went into military service. In Iran, draft is mandatory. He was given six months of ordinary military period, and the rest of his service time was spent in an office. He was the son of the secretary of war, so he was allowed to take his beloved Porsche with him to the base!

He also had, tailor-made, two military suits that were two sizes too big for him! It was a dirty green suit. He would spend the whole week on the base, and on weekends, he would come home to the basement and me. I was double uncomfortable living in my in-laws' house and no privacy without my husband. Bahman's logic was, since your parents got divorced and were not happy together, it's good for you to live with my parents and learn what a happy home is about! Yeah. No mention of him being a mama's boy, and he justified his behavior toward me!

Writing about Bahman's military suit reminds me of a wedding I attended. My Uncle's wife's brother was the groom, and Bahman joined me later at the party wearing his military clothes, while everybody was wearing long dresses for the wedding party!

Neither the two rooms next to the pool, which we lived in for the first two months upon our return, nor the basement had a kitchen. But the basement had no door to the outside either. In order to go outside, one had to pass in front of everybody's eyes after you climbed the steps. I was a total prisoner under the surveillance of all. I never invited my parents, sister, or friends over. I did not dare invite them, as I felt this was not my house. It was theirs, and I was a guest in the basement.

Also, I did not notice that, although I lived in Tehran, I was never hearing the radio or TV in Farsi because Bahman did not like it.

I never saw our wedding picture on their mantel or anywhere in the house. I was told that, unless I became a Baha'i, in their eyes, I was not married. But Bahman himself at that time showed no interest in declaring himself as a Baha'i and hated religion, and I had no choice in that.

I felt unwanted and different, and I had no privacy. It bothered me that my husband was so dependent on his family. He would not spend money on me, and up to this day, I don't know how much he made. If his parents spent money, he thought he was spending it. He had no sense of "we" as a separate family from his parents.

The only guest we ever had was my aunt who was minister of education and her husband, General Shirin Sokhan. His parents did not receive my relatives in their beautiful guest room with golden partitions imported from Harrods of England but, rather, next to the pool on the porch of the two rooms. How humiliating .

Actually, all the years I knew them, that room was opened once, and that was when my son was born, and all his family were invited. I was not allowed to go in the room, as I guess some Baha'i ceremony and blessings from them were performed. I was left outside the guest room, and they brought my baby back to me to breastfeed him. That really hurt me.

Bahman finished his military service and started a job in a newly founded office called the Development and Advancement of Industry of Iran. I was busy with my new job as an IBM programmer with a bunch of other young graduates, but I figured the company wanted too much from us. They said, "You live to work." And I said, "You work to live." So I preferred to live. The company planned classes at night and this and that. I went home and told Bahman, and he suggested that I complain. I did and was fired. The company wanted me to put my job first and my life second.

From there, I went to work for a planning and budget organization. It was located way downtown of Tehran, and I was working as a computer specialist. We took special classes, and I met people who, even after the revolution, I met up with again in the United States. Small world.

But before that, something happened. And it convinced Bahman to move out of that basement. (We moved, however, still one street away from his parents. And every day we visited them and even bought bread for them every other day, although they had two servants and a chauffeur.)

CHAPTER 17

GETTING OUR OWN ONE BEDROOM APARTMENT, 1976–1977

Bahman's parents had two German shepherds called Chicho and Niki. Chicho was crazy and would even bite the hand of whoever fed him, let alone others. I was very scared of these two dogs. Their house was set on an acre, and on top of the hill was a greenhouse. One day, I was walking with Bahman up there to look at the flowers, and on my way back, I heard the breathing of the dogs. They were running toward me and I was screaming and quite shaken. Bahman and the gardener took them, and I ran to the basement crying.

Later on, we found out Maryam and Amir had let the dogs loose knowing I was up there. Maryam came to the basement for the first time and kneeled in front of Bahman and started apologizing. Hello. I am the one who was attacked and scared. Why was she apologizing to Bahman? She totally ignored me and asked Bahman to forgive her. Something happened, and Bahman agreed we should start looking for a house.

A relative's husband, Farrokh (the husband of Nahid, my aunt's daughter), suggested a one-bedroom apartment that his brother's wife, an Italian called Chichi, owned. It was very small but pretty clean.

Timsar said, "People live in cabins on a ship. Size is not important."

I was happy to gain some privacy, and I guess the apartment's best feature, to Bahman and his family's eyes, was its location—only two minutes from his parents'. We were at Fereshteh Street in Elahieh, and they were at Maghsoud Beyk Street, also in Elahieh. We moved there and started our half-private life, still visiting his parents at least every other day.

I agreed to give all of my salary to Bahman, and he would take care of rent and food with my salary and his. I never saw his paychecks, but he saw all of mine and knew how much I made. I was an observer, obedient throughout the whole marriage. Just like in my childhood games I had been allowed to be only an observant per my mother's instructions. Maybe that was why I didn't feel that it was an odd place to be in a marriage. Any decision made for our life was made by him—this included our married life; my health; and, later on, decisions about our child and what he ate and wore.

I was thinking of divorce and, at the same time, hoping for a solution. I still liked Bahman and wanted him to see for himself that this was not a joined married life— that his family was a separate entity from us. But all things were in his hands, done by sweetness, kindness, laughter, and all of the other characteristics he outwardly displayed.

Life went on, and we were happier in that little apartment. But we only slept there. And for a variety of reasons or none at all, we ended up eating and being with his family and the big yard and chef and grills.

After a year, Maryam got pregnant and went to England to deliver her baby, called Behzad. Her mother followed her to be with her. We accompanied Bahman's father so he would not be alone.

I again changed my job and went to the Cultural Affairs of the Court, where we developed a computer package with the help of a computer organization called ISIRAN and the "digital" computer company. The computer program was documenting all movements of the Shah, retrievable by key words. Whether he gave a speech or was in a ceremony opening a new organization, whatever he said was stored in the computer, with key words enabling its retrieval. The idea was like Google or the hashtag (#) functionality. This was making the history of Iran retrievable.

Once, my car broke down, and Bahman took me to work in his Porsche. All my coworkers were awed and thought how lucky and happy I must be. Never judge a book by its cover.

I could not consult my mother because she was happy, having achieving her goals of having a daughter who was educated and had married an engineer from a good family. I asked my sister whether she was happy in her marriage. I remember I was telling my sister how unhappy I felt, and she said, "Stop complaining. Have a child, and it will get better."

So I started trying to get pregnant and, at the same time, hoping one of us had a problem and could not produce a child. I would then have a good reason for a divorce. Deep in my heart, I was afraid of his father and family. They were so influential in Iran. If they did not agree with my divorce, might they harm us? Go figure.

CHAPTER 18

GETTING PREGNANT, 1976

One day, I imitated what I had seen in a movie. For getting pregnant, one should put her legs up after making love. I did that. The next day, I regretted it and thought, *Who guarantees that by having a baby things will get better?*

I told my coworker, Mrs. Saee, that, when I got my period that month, I would get a divorce. I wasn't happy when I missed my period and went to a lab to test my urine for pregnancy. When I was informed that the lab was more than 100 percent sure that I was pregnant, I did not smile. I was too religious to abort a baby, so I thought I would stay as long as I was breastfeeding the baby—or, as my religion said, when the child was over two years old. If things improved during that period, I would stay. I would never leave before that or while I was breastfeeding. I did not know a revolution was shaping in Iran and lots of other decisions were being made behind my back by my husband's family. I also did not understand the strong love of motherhood after the baby is born that I would have to deal with throughout my whole life.

I came home and announced my pregnancy. Bahman took control of everything and said, "You stop reading anything about pregnancy because you will get all the symptoms you read about." He was the one reading the books and observing me, and if I showed any signs of anything, he would know what to do.

I would throw up in the mornings right after I went to the bathroom. The only unusual thing that happened to me was that, one day, I was cutting a chicken to make lunch and a very weird feeling came over me as I was cutting the meat of a live thing. The smell and the feeling were so strong that I dropped the knife, and I said, "I will never cut any chicken as long as I live." Bahman took over that part of cooking. Of course I got back to normal after I gave birth.

Also I was craving these incredibly sour lemon pickles that an Indian friend of Bahman introduced us to. I still love them and wish I had the recipe. I followed Bahman—carried out all his plans, took on all his friends, and adopted his lifestyle and decisions.

Once, Dr. Nahavandi told Bahman as we were getting ready to go in his Porsche and I was very pregnant, "Be careful. You are carrying a very breakable cargo, just like glass." He wanted him to drive more slowly until I gave birth.

My mother and I flew to Germany to buy special orange and yellow beds and a bath set for my baby. I don't think Bahman's family pitched in for that. At that time, the gender of the baby was unknown, and I had to buy orange and yellow to go with any gender. We were still in the one-bedroom apartment, and life was the same. As I was getting closer to my delivery date, the doctor took an x-ray and found the baby was too big for me. I was scared of the scar I had on my tummy from the two operations I'd had and thought I would burst open one day. I did not know that, by ignoring my tummy and not looking at it, it would not grow less. Also, I could see that, when I sat down, the tummy would go right and left, and the poor baby had not much room to maneuver.

Giving birth to Babak, my son, 1977

The first time I heard my baby's heart beat, I fell in love with him. It was a very strange feeling, very emotional. I was carrying another live creature inside me—a little angel. One day, as I was cleaning the apartment, I felt a pain. I called my mother and said I think I hurt my back when I moved the furniture; I have a backache. My mother called back after she'd consulted my aunt, who was a physician, and she said I should immediately check into the hospital. I asked Bahman to please not tell anyone until I was out of the delivery room. Also I did not want him to be present when I gave birth. I was not at ease going to the bathroom without complete privacy, let alone giving birth while all are were watching me. He assured me he would not. But he called his parents and my mother as soon as he could and asked them to stay put till later.

We went to the hospital, and I was told the opening or dilation was not large enough. So I was checked into a room. They also asked me to stay in the room to separate me from another expectant mother, who was as dilated as I was but was making such a fuss and screaming that the doctors thought it better if I were not next to her. Bahman and I very slowly walked up the hospital corridor. As soon as I entered my room, I felt something very hot running down my legs. My water had broken. So we walked all the way back to the labor room. And by that time, a new patient was there.

She and I would get our pains at exactly the same time—I mean to the second. There I found out that God had planted a clock down there for women, and mine was synced to this woman next to me. She had the accent of the people from Mashad, northeast of Iran, a religious city. She would shout, "O Imam Reza, I am dying." I was just sitting down when I had my pain. For some reason, they took her to the operating room, but I was there the whole night.

Early in the morning, as soon as my doctor, Dr. Adl, arrived, I took him by his tie and demanded a C-section. I was tired, had not slept the whole night, and could not take it any longer. The doctor ordered the nurses to prepare me for the operation. I heard someone say, "Oh, her water broke, and she has negative RH. I hope the baby is not blue," or something to that extent.

I was worried and did not understand what they meant. I was still awake when the nurse told the doctor to go ahead. I said, "Not yet!"

The doctor told the nurse, "That is very dangerous if you are not sure—"

Then I passed out.

I woke up to my mother telling me, "Congratulations. You have a boy."

I was shivering like crazy. I supposed that was normal. I asked, "Where is the baby?"

I heard the strangest reply. "You cannot see or hold the baby until twenty-four hours has passed!"

What on earth did they mean I couldn't see the baby? Bahman said he had seen the baby and had held him. I called the nurse and said, "Can I just see him from afar?" I bribed her with a gold coin, and she brought the baby's basket and left it at the corner of the room. I was not allowed to touch or breastfeed him for twenty-four hours.

Later in life, I read somewhere that the bond happens when the mother holds the baby in the first twenty-four hours. Who knew about that? But, thank God, I had a C-section. And as soon as the baby is born, the doctors put the baby on the mother's tummy, and that push brings the placenta out too—something someone did not calculate.

I took a picture of my new baby with his beautiful red lips while I cried. He was a beautiful baby. I understood not being able to breastfeed him, as I was taking antibiotics. But not holding him? Who had given that order? When I showed the picture later on that day to my uncle Farhang, he said "These lips are too red. It's photoshopped." And we laughed. I took it with my own Polaroid camera that Bahman had used to take pictures of me while I was pregnant. Later on, the pictures were confiscated by Khomeini guards after the revolution.

Anyway, that weird event passed, and the next day as I was sitting in the hospital room with Bahman, the nurse came and said, "Do you want to breastfeed the baby?"

I said, "Yes, but do I have milk?"

She squeezed my breast. And, wow, there came milk. One of the miracles of God is that red blood changes to white milk and is the only food a baby can have, and it was running in my veins. The second miracle was holding my baby. He immediately sucked my breast and knew what to do. It hurt a lot to breastfeed after a C-section, but I was happy to be allowed to hold him and touch him and sing lullabies for him.

I was thinking of two names, Babak, which was a hero's name, and Shervin, which was a new name used by the young generation. Somehow Babak won out, and his name became Babak Joon, meaning Dear Babak. He was so pretty and so much of a good baby it was amazing.

I think the rest of my story should be written by Shakespeare, as the tragedy of the love of a mother for her son and their separation is not describable. I was hoping our new son would bring a change to our life. But I found out that I was, again, an observant, and all others were raising my son and making decisions about every aspect of my child's life.

CHAPTER 19

RETURNING HOME FROM THE HOSPITAL AFTER GIVING BIRTH, 1977

I moved to my mother's house after giving birth, as the doctor explained that I needed attention for at least three months after the surgery. But in one day, Bahman's mother came over with a bunch of plastic bowls and baths. She claimed our house was not clean enough for the baby! Bahman said we should move back to our little apartment. I was left alone with no help and no mother and sister to help me so that I would not confront my husband.

Bahman's mother would visit us and give Babak a bath. I would breastfeed him. I complained about the one bedroom being so small, and they agreed that we could move one street down into a two-bedroom with steps that led to the second floor. This house had no privacy either, as the one tenant living downstairs shared the steps with us and could hear everything we said.

I was happy to have a room for the child. But one day, after having a cold, I almost fell down the steps and passed out. When I recovered I saw myself lying on the floor of the kitchen, Babak in a carriage next to me, and Bahman putting water on my face. I guess the nervous system could not take it any longer. He agreed we would move back to the other building where we'd had the one-bedroom unit and rent a two-bedroom apartment with no steps in it.

All the time I was trying to convince him that we could afford to buy a house, since we both worked and were graduates of good schools in the United States. But Bahman could not separate his life completely from his parents. He still lives close to his mother, who is now ninety-one, and visits her often, while he has a wife and a child in Canada—the great mama's boy.

Going to San Francisco and Texas with Babak and Mother, 1977

When my son, was a few months old, Bahman was sent on a mission to San Francisco through the Bechtel Company, an American engineering company. Iran was going strong in all areas thanks to the oil money. The country had a king and a queen who were advanced in education and planning and had dreams for Iran's future. I was torn between which system worked better—a monarchy or a republic.

At any rate, my mother accompanied us on this trip, and we all stayed in San Francisco for a while, when Babak could not yet walk. When I got off the plane with Babak and Mother, Bahman and an American gentleman were awaiting us. It is a long trip from Iran to the United States—more than twelve hours, and you wear comfortable clothes with a baby accompanying you. Bahman was angry with me because I was not dressed formally in front of that high-ranking Bechtel employee.

After a couple of days and me falling in love with Santa Cruz, Babak and Mother and I went to Texas to visit my brother Farzad. He was waiting for his wife, Roya, who he'd just married and lived there. On that trip, I did not dare tell my mother how unhappy I had been for years.

We returned, and Bahman's family decided that we should have a Filipino maid and nurse taking care of Babak while I went back to work. At that time, the dollar was so strong in Iran that even foreign countries' teachers would come to Iran to work as a maid and send their money back to their families in the Philippines. For example, one dollar was 7.5 toomans (750 rials) before the revolution in Iran, and now one dollar is 16,000 toomans (160,000 rials). We were all at Bahman's parents' house when Mrs. Yamini, one of Amir's relatives, told me to go to the Filipino embassy and tell them, "I want one of those girls you keep in the back."

I did, and I saw the guy jump from his seat when I said it. I guess it was a code, and something was special about those girls in the back, as opposed to other girls brought to Iran as au pairs to take care of the babies of the young and educated population of Iran at that time. Well, he returned with a girl called Angela who was a little on the heavy side. She was supposed to live with us and take care of Babak when I went to work. She spoke English well and said she was a teacher back in the Philippines. She also said she had never been married.

We divided Babak's room with a partition, designating a third of the room as hers, and she lived in Babak's room. I started going back to work. And at ten o'clock, I would lactate wherever I was—in a meeting or in the bathroom or in my office—and had to hide it with lots of tissues. Why society turns a deaf ear to this natural act of women when they are granted equality is still a wonder to me. How do men live with their consciences?

I learned years and years later that, when I was at work, Bahman's mother would send the driver to fetch Angela and Babak to her house. There she would get a massage from Angela, and then she would feed and bathe Babak, all behind my back. Sometimes I would give the child another bath without knowing what had happened. I also did not know what he ate and how much. I was purposely kept in the dark about anything and everything related to our married life, even my child.

CHAPTER 20

PLANS MADE BEHIND MY BACK, 1979

Yes, I had plans to leave. But after my child was born, I found out how difficult it would be to leave him. However, two things happened that made the decision for me—the revolution that threatened the Baha'i and a plan made behind my back by Bahman and his family for the whole family to migrate to Canada.

One day, Bahman came home and dropped the bomb. He said, "We are planning to go to Canada and live there." The Canadian embassy wouldn't let Babak travel without the mother's permission. Thank you, Canada, for being so considerate of women's rights. In Iran, the rule was that, at the time of divorce, the boy goes to the father when he is two and the girl when she is seven. My son was close to two years old. We were not talking of divorce yet, and I was extremely surprised and hurt. But as usual, I kept quiet. In my mind I said, *Where was I when all his family were discussing this subject? Why am I just an observer? This is not a decision made in a day or two. Also how come they never invite my parents to their house?*

My friends would tell me they would have divorced their husbands a long time ago if their in-laws didn't invite their parents to their house, knowing that I lived with them for a good while too.

I don't know why I'm this way. I accept and keep quiet until one day I burst and say goodbye. The same type of outburst happened between me and my sister, which I will explain later. I should have let the anger come out slowly and started demanding. But that is my character. I usually say, if the other person knew better, he or she would not try to hurt me so much. I forgive till my anger explodes.

I may have asked Bahman, "Where was I when you and your parents and Maryam and Amir were discussing the migration to Canada? Did anybody ask me whether I wanted to go to another country, where the only people I would know would be just my in-laws again?"

On the other hand, since his family were Baha'i—even today, forty years later, in Iran, those who are Baha'i are captured, have no right to go to Iranian universities, and so forth and so on—I had to think of the safety of my child. I signed my permission for his travel while I was hurt, angry, and had no other choice. Revolution was happening so quickly.

There is this stupid law created after the 1979 Revolution that has been in place for forty years now. It holds that a boy, until age two and a girl until age seven belongs to the mother. After that, the law gives the child to the father. So my child, being a boy. was automatically given to his father at the time of our divorce, and I had no power over it. I am very angry with that law, which is both discriminative against women and utterly illogical. But some learn to abide, especially after a fresh revolution that was a so-called religious one.

We planned a trip to Gajereh to ski. On top of the hill when I touched the snow with my skis, I could not hold onto my silence anymore. I told Bahman, first, I wanted a divorce and, second, I could not take one more step. He called the guards, and this man who would carry the injured put me on a barricade and took me down the hill. That trip was soooo long for me. I made a decision, closed my eyes, and let God take me to a new destiny. I thought, *I am making a good decision for my son's safety. They are taking him to Canada anyway.* From now on, if I stay, he will see fights between his parents and infidelities. I knew how painful the fights of parents are for a child. My parents constantly fought and divorced three times. I did not want my son to go through that.

That was my logic—on top of my system crashing and not taking this weird arrangement of constantly living with in-laws, having no decisions about our future made between me and my husband but, rather, between Bahman and his parents and sister. That was not my way of life. I thought my son would have a quieter life and a happier one if I left before we get to the fighting stage. I did not know how difficult life would be without my son—how much I would miss him, how I would become a zombie and make wrong decisions. I was young, unhappy, and angry that I had no control over any part of my life. My son, our future, where we lived, what properties we bought—all was decided by them. I also did not predict that his father and I would each have another divorce, and he would see more divorces. If I knew the future, I would have kept quiet—would have continued never ever saying a word until he was eighteen.

We went to the court. He said his mother had gotten a lawyer. And I told him to save that money. I want nothing except to have contact with my son, to know of his whereabouts, and to be granted visitations. I asked to see him every weekend—a request that was granted. Who gets the child was decided by the laws in Iran, which meant the child went to the father. But usually, the father would give the child to the mother.

I also knew that soon they would leave for Canada, so I asked to be allowed to see him once a year—with expenses paid by them. They *never* honored that arrangement, and I had to pay for every visit. I did not get a penny as alimony or anything else but had to pay for plane tickets to see my son for one month out of the year. The weekend visits and once a month per year became days per year, most the time less than a week.

Other events changed these arrangements too, like the American hostage taking of Iran, no visas issued to Iranians, and the Iran-Iraq War. My destiny was to just have temporary visits. My life and choices after that were lived and made with a broken heart. I was living like a zombie, like I'd faced Sophie's choice, like *Kramer vs. Kramer*, like an ocean of black sorrow.

Meanwhile the revolution was brewing in Iran. I moved to my mother's house.

When I returned to my parents' house after my divorce, I saw that they had made an arrangement. Mamnan Zinat Joon was living in a studio with a sunny kitchen and bathroom facilities at a corner of my mother and uncle Farhang's house. My uncle's wife, Sorayajoon, took care of her daily. Grandma was sweet to all and would indulge in her hookah. My son called her Mammon Atish, since *atish* means fire, referring to the charcoal on top of her hookah. There I lived for a while with her, since Mother went to America. That was when I got power of attorney from both Mother and my sister to transfer my mother's apartment in Farmanieh of Tehran to my sister, Shahla's, name.

CHAPTER 21

LIVING WITH MY SISTER, GRANDMA, AND MOTHER, 1979–1981

Later on, my sister returned from Germany with her beautiful daughter. The rumor was that her husband was having an affair with a German woman and the woman was pregnant with a son.

From then on, she and her daughter, along with my grandmother and I, would pass the horrifying moments of the Iran-Iraq War together. Once I was asked to go get the daughter from her school, since both my sister and Soraya Joon, my uncle's wife were busy and could not go get her. As soon as the school bell rang and all kids started leaving the school, I started crying hard, thinking of my son and who would be bringing him back from school. As of that day, they decided that I should not be around any children. In the United States, too, this continued. I would not be invited or go to any parties because I would cry and remember my son. It wasn't as if he was not constantly on my mind, but this interaction would trigger a nerve that would render me unable to stop crying.

I also remember that we were supposed to put black tape on the windows so they would not break when the planes flew low. And once we were told to go to a place with no widows around when we heard a "red" siren. Once, we were all sitting in one part of our house. My sister was crying and holding her daughter. My grandma sat next to me and prayed. We closed the doors of the rooms and bathroom so we were surrounded by doors, not windows. I looked up and saw this huge hanging lamp above our heads. If it was shaken and broken, it would throw glass on us more than a window! It took a long time before the "green" siren was heard, and we all hugged each other and tried to act normal again.

My uncle and his family were doing the same one floor below us. We were on the second floor, and they were on the first floor. I heard later that they would go to the basement from then on.

That war took eight years and lots of casualty. That war changed my perspective on life.

CHAPTER 22

TAKEN ADVANTAGE OF IN BERLIN, 1980

Since after my son left I felt so miserable and could not function well, I planned to wait till Bahman and his family got to Canada and got situated there. Then I would go and get a job there and find a house near them. I did not know that life had other plans for me. I had to leave Iran sooner, and at the time, they were in Switzerland, a country I'd never visited, with languages I knew nothing about. Because of the event in Berlin that I will explain in this chapter, along with the fact that American hostages were taken by Iran, getting a visa was so difficult that I had to go wherever I was accepted. And in each country, I had to start my life from zero.

The first event that led to this path was this unexpected and unbelievable event. When I went to help my sister, I got bitten for the rest of my life. All my relatives left me when I told them this part of my story twenty years later, punishing me, the victim, as opposed to the wrongdoer.

I am writing about one of the biggest mistakes of my life.

First, I need to explain my sister. My sister and I are totally different. She loved to play with dolls. I did not. Her dolls had great dresses. Mine did not. She was curious about relationships between men and women, and I was not. She was calculating, and maybe that was why she became an accountant later. I was straightforward. She was a planner and politician. I was not. She was not sensitive, and killing a cat with a car would not make her cry. But it did have a great affect and sadness on me. She loves a man no matter what. I love with conditions. She was singing and listening to jokes on the radio when I was first visiting my father's grave. I was crying and she was indifferent because she had her emotions the year before when he actually died but had no consideration of my emotions. I begged her once to take me to see my grandpa in the hospital, and she did not. She had no emotions except for those toward her own husband and family. To me, she was as different from me as day is from night. She is not a considerate woman in my book because she accepted anything a man did to her—from having affairs to taking advantage of her own sister.

She did arrange my meeting with her husband, as I had no address or phone number to get in touch with him. And when I managed to bring him back to Iran, she started denying the whole thing. She had control over friends and family and forced all of them to leave me. I have scars in my heart left by my sister as deep as a valley.

I was under thirty years old when I separated from Bahman, and I immediately moved to my mother's house. My mother was out of Iran at that time. My grandmother lived in the same house with us, although she'd had a studio built for her at the end of the yard. It was during the Iran-Iraq War and the beginning of the revolution too. At one point, Shahla and her only child at the time, Sepideh, came back to Iran from Germany. She was sad and crying a lot. Her husband was having an affair with a German woman, and they had separated, though not officially. I'd planned a long time before that to go to Rome in Italy and Holland. I got fed up seeing my sister cry every day and also over the fact that we heard that the German woman had gotten pregnant. So as I was too young and thought I could solve the matter, I volunteered to add an extra night into my trip and go to Berlin to see what he was up to.

My sister made the arrangements for me to go there and informed her husband, Mehrdad, of my flight time and date. I had no phone number or address for him as my sister was, as usual, controlling everything. I did not know that lots of men were waiting to get their hands on a young and pretty and educated young woman like me. The last person I would have thought of thinking that way was him. In my book, he was zero, and now he is minus.

At any rate, I flew to Berlin, and he came to the airport to pick me up. My acquaintance with him was very limited. I'd seen him only on a few occasions, when I'd gone to Germany with my mother or at family gatherings. So I thought he might show some respect. Also, I had plans to pretend I was friendly with him so that maybe he would show me the German woman and I could see how their relation was and how far into pregnancy she was. As I was waiting for my suitcases to arrive, I peeked outside to see whether he'd come to pick me up with her or whether he was alone. I saw him and got so angry that I turned red and quickly turned my back. I figured this would be harder than I'd imagined, since I hated what he was doing—having an affair and leaving his wife and little daughter alone with no money or anything and having fun with a new woman.

I practiced a smile and went out. On the road to his house, the address of which I didn't know—neither did I know his phone number, and I could only speak a very limited German—I asked him, "What are you doing these day?"

He said, "I have become an actor and am acting most of the time." It was a sarcastic answer, as he was not truly sharing any information about his life.

We got to his house and I asked, "Where is this German girlfriend of yours? I heard you have one?"

He poured some wine and said something to divert my attention.

I said, "Can we go to a bar or a restaurant and ask her to come and we'll all meet up?"

He said, "No. I'd rather be with you alone." Then he dropped the bomb and said, "I always loved you from the day I came to ask for your sister's hand."

My shock was so obvious that he started laughing. I said, "Are you joking?"

He said, "I swear."

I got scared—OMG, what am I getting myself into? I thought of first calling the police. Well, first there were no cell phones, and then I did not know the number for the German police. I still don't. Plus I did not know his address to give to the police. I was totally in his hands. If I wanted to make a call, he would have to dial the number for me.

I changed my plan and I said, "I am tired. Where do I sleep?"

"On the floor," he told me, though there was a couch and a small rug.

I don't remember his house. I don't want to remember anything. But when something happens or a word is spoken, it is impossible to take it back from your memory. I just knew that he had me alone in a captured situation and would take advantage of me. I had always practiced in my mind that, if anyone wanted to rape me, I would submit. I heard rapists love it when you fight. All I could do was take the pleasure out of it for him. That was all I could do. I was even at his mercy to take me back to the airport. I just lay there and submitted. I only asked him, "If I agree, will you come back to Iran, since you claim you love me so much?"

He said, "Yes I will."

He was thinking that he would come back to Iran and start a relationship with me, and I was thinking about how to free myself from that house.

He was so much of an ass that he even said, "Oh, you are like a hen—no feelings."

I was so angry with him that he expected me to enjoy it. You are my sister's husband and the lover of a pregnant German woman who you're having an affair with. How much lower do you want to get?

I had relations before but I wanted it. This was a rape since I did not want it to happen. I will hate him always to the day I die. What happened next was that, around 4:00 a.m., my sister called the cousin of her husband and asked him to come to his house. As he rang the bell, I felt so happy and so brave. He walked in, and I immediately asked him to take me to the airport. Mehrdad, my sister's unfaithful husband, had to shut up because a third person was present.

I said, "See you," and left.

I wanted him to go to Iran, and then my father, as a judge, and Mahmud Khan, a relative and lawyer, would get alimony from him and get my sister's divorce. My plan was to leave Iran.

I have stayed away from him for thirty years now. I don't know if I'll ever see him before I die, but I would love to hit him hard. I've tried to forgive, but I can't forget. Now the worst thing that happened was that I thought that, as soon as I told my sister that her husband had an eye on me, she would leave him. But no, she ignored all my comments and even was happy that it meant he did not love the

German woman and to hell with her own sister. All I could do was to not let him see me as much as possible because he was staying in the family.

Mother returned from abroad. I will explain what I did later because the next event overshadows all the events in our lives.

CHAPTER 23

THE DAY IN MAY: MY AUNT'S ARREST AND EXECUTION, 1980

The capture and execution of my aunt as the first woman in the Shah's cabinet was awaiting us. I first described the events in detail years ago, and I submitted that article to a political publication, *Azadi*. It's included in the political life section of this book. But now I write it as a personal diary entry.

After my aunt was captured by Khomeini's guards, her husband, General Shirin Sokhan; her son, Hamid; her, daughter, Mahshid; and, once, my mother would visit her in prison. On the day my mother went, I wondered, *Why am I not allowed to go see my aunt?* But I was happy that my cousin Mahshid, who was pregnant, was going to see her. She was supposed to come from the south of Iran any minute on a day that would turn tragic to visit her mother. I was worried for her, since she was in her last months of pregnancy, and flying is not good at that time.

On that same day, I had to see a friend of my uncle, Mr. Shariff, to exchange some currency. He was in the bazaar. News was always spread there first, and from there it would make it through the upper-class part of the city. Mr. Shariff came in, and after we did the money exchange, I said something in regard to being worried for my aunt, since at 8:00 a.m., the list of names of those who were executed had not been announced on the radio. (It was customary that, in the morning, around 8:00 a.m., a list of those who had been executed earlier that day would be announced.)

Mr. Shariff reacted with great surprise. "Did you not hear? They had a firing squad for her."

I was completely numb, but I said, "No. Her son, Hamid, and her husband, Timsar, saw her last night."

Mr. Shariff left in a hurry. And as I was getting myself together, the phone rang. It was Nasi Amir, my high school best friend. She said her mother had passed out on the couch when she heard the news.

I said, "No. It's not true. We saw her last night, and they are going today to see her. My cousin is flying in today from the south of Iran to see her."

As soon as I hung up the phone, Kourosh, my uncle's son who lived on the first floor of the building where we lived on the second floor, walked into our house and said, "They hit her."

These words will stick in my ears forever.

Then Soraya Joon, my uncle Farhang's wife walked in. I remember, my mother; Soraya Joon; my grandma, Mammon Zinat Joon; and I were all sitting on the floor of the kitchen, and once in a while, one of us would sigh. We were all shocked, grief-stricken, numb, in disbelief, and in deep sorrow. I don't know how much time passed, but my mother got up and said, "We have to go to their house and break the news, so they won't go to the prison to visit."

I said, "I'll come with you."

We both dressed in black, hoping they would guess when they saw us. Who could deliver such news? We did not notice that my maternal grandma could not speak a word due to the shock. She was in that state for the next three days.

My mother and I tried to compose ourselves. We walked into the yard of my aunt's house. Hamid was still upstairs getting ready and was waiting for Mahshid to arrive so they could all go to see their mother in prison. Timsar started telling us how he'd met her last night and how they had a pardon letter from Prime Minister Bani Sadr and she would be freed soon with the letter.

My mother figured they did not notice our black clothes or sad faces. My mother said, "Why don't you wait until General Malek Ahmadi" (the father of their son-in-law, Farrokh) "gets here. He has the latest news."

Hamid walked down the stairs and asked, "What happened?"

I turned to him and could not hold back tears any more.

At that moment, general Malek Ahmadi walked into the yard, his face soaked in tears and cried, mumbling something. Seeing him Timsar and Hamid understood. I ran and hugged Hamid. We cried.

Hamid said, "I will kill them, the *pasdars*, the dirty Khomeini guards."

In my heart, I said, *I will help you if I can.*

We knew we were helpless; they had power, were armed, and had no mercy.

At that moment, General Shirin Sokhan, my aunt's husband, took charge of everything. He became the mother, father, guardian, grandma, and grandpa of their family. Timsar, my aunt's husband, had already proven his noble manhood by accepting his wife holding a position higher than his. Rarely would men do that, especially in that culture. Of course, we found out that he could not pee for several days as one of the reactions to such grave news and injustice.

The next immediate thing to do was to tell Mahshid, my pregnant cousin, that she couldn't go to the prison to visit her mother anymore. Hamid said, "I will do it. You all stay in this room quietly."

We heard Mahshid walking from the narrow alley into the kitchen. It was quiet for a while, and then we heard Mahshid crying and shouting, "No, no, no!"

I ran into the kitchen and hugged her. We all joined in and cried. I made sure I stay with Mahshid all the time, since she was pregnant.

Timsar said he would send the chauffeur to the prison to see whether we could get the body. At that time, the regime would sometimes charge you for the bullets they used to frighten and humiliate you even more. They would not let you formally bury those they executed. So much cruelty was going on after the revolution that we could expect anything.

While we were waiting, I took Mahshid to our house so she would not hear Hamid's wife, Manige, who'd just arrived, and was so shocked she was saying things like, "Oh, they will throw her body to us and will have no respect." I did not want Mahshid, being pregnant, to bear more sorrow.

Once we got to our house, the phone rang. It was Nahid, my cousin and Mahshid's sister, calling from California to get some news. I gave the phone to

Mahshid. She mumbled something and gave the phone back to me. I had to say it. I said, "We are waiting for some news, but it seems like they have done it."

Up to this day, Nahid says that, every time she talks to me on the phone, she hears those words—the same as every time I talk to Kourosh, my cousin, I hear the same words. I was the messenger of the worst news anyone could hear.

I returned with Mahshid to their house. The chauffeur, Nejati, arrived. He had some of my aunt's belongings, among them her prayer materials. I found out later her effects included a letter, like her will; a ring; and a watch. I did not know the content but dreamed of a ring she gave to me to give to Mahshid that night. I will explain this in more detail in another chapter later.

I only add the will she wrote during the final hours of her life here. The translation of Dr. Farrokh Rou Parsay (my aunt's) last will:

> In the name of God [this phrase she was forced by the executors to write], I don't have a last will because I don't have much equity, and whatever I did have was confiscated from me [by the regime of Iran]. I don't owe anyone anything, and if I someone owes me anything, that person can give it to my children.
>
> I know, and my conscience is clear, that whatever accusations are made about me and written about me are false and not done by me.
>
> My prayer stuff and the rosary and my ring and watch should be given to my husband to give to my daughter. And whatever else I have in the prison I will donate to Fatemeh Pour Yousefian (her prison guard).
>
> This court differentiates vastly between men and women, and I hope the future of women will be better than this.
>
> The money that I have in prison should be divided between the prisoners.

This document was signed by my aunt, Dr. Parsay, who wrote and signed . She had no fear whatsoever. That makes me admire her even more. There is no visible shake of the hand that wrote these final words. I accept her as one of the primary leaders in the struggle for women's liberation. The same respect goes for my grandmother Fakhr Afagh Parsay. Both were pioneers in the history of Iran and, for that matter, the world's struggle among women to gain equality with men in the law.

CHAPTER 24

PERIOD, PREGNANCY, CHILDBIRTH, BREASTFEEDING

The world tries to sweep the natural event of a woman having her period every month under the rug, and there are no laws written on what to do with women during their period. However, I witnessed a change. Just in Iran, in 1978, the head of our HR department at Iran Electronics Industry (affiliated with Iran's Ministry of Defence), a woman called Malihe, made a rule that each woman in the office under the age of sixty could take one day off as paid leave for her period. I loved that.

If more companies did that, then the world would notice how slowly it was advancing when it is still taboo to talk about a woman's period. The subject is not mentioned anywhere in the thick documents of the vast majority of company's HR departments. Not one word about women's periods can be found among them.

We need lots of laws about women added to the current laws all over the world—laws about pregnancy, breastfeeding, periods, and whatever else a woman goes through that a man does not. How long do we have to wait to see the rules made for human beings, not just for men?

That cause has always been number one in my life, especially as I always had very painful periods. I missed events, weddings, and parties due to my situation, which I share with millions of other women. I could not travel for a couple of days due to heavy bleeding. But in spite of that and with difficulty, I worked all my life and made my living expenses and paid for my son's trips or helped a little with his school loans if I could. I wish the world would wake up and changes lots of rules, taking women into consideration. When will that become a priority? When the world is ruled by women?

CHAPTER 25

MY MOTHER AND FATHER

Before I continue the story, I have to introduce you to my parents. And in doing that, I may jump ahead and come back to 1981, the time I left Iran to see my son after a year of separation. But life does not wait for one event to finish to start another. It always has lots of events and changes unfolding parallel to each other.

One of the hard chapters to write about for me is describing my mother. She was loved by all and was beautiful. But we had to witness her angry side, because life did not treat her well. She worked both outside and inside of the house every day of her life. She did not have a happy marriage and went through three divorces with the same man, our father. She gave birth to four children. My sister was the eldest and then I came along after three years, and my two brothers were born after that, each two years apart.

I remember my mother complaining about my father constantly. and she had a right to most of the time. She came from a family that very politely and respectfully obeyed the rules of the society. But when she brought dowry, which in Farsi is said *jahaz* (a word that also refers to the camel's hump), my father said, "Well, a camel has a hump too." My father's side of the family was considered intellectual and educated. My father was twenty and was studying law (he would later become a prosecutor, which we call a judge in Iran), and my mother was seventeen or even sixteen when they met. Since my father was short and my mother was tall, she looked older than my father in their wedding pictures.

This young couple loved each other a lot, but neither was skillful enough to manage a married life. And they went through lots of fights that we children were the daily witnesses of. In my opinion, damage was done to all four of us as a result, even if we deny it.

They either lovingly adored each other or were each other's enemies. So many times we heard from my mother, "If it weren't for these four kids, I would have left." And thus, we felt guilty for having been born.

Or she would recite this famous poetry in Iran that would translate to, "In the end, the one born from a wolf becomes a wolf, even if he or she is raised by humans." The wolf was my father, and the human was my mother! My father's name became "that low-level being"(*bisharafe bi pedar madar*). And if they were in their loving phase, she called him Pouri, the abbreviation of Farrokh Pour. We did not bring our school friends to our house when they were together, as we were uncomfortable in front of friends, in case they started a fight.

All this affected my mother, causing her to be an angry person. She never kissed us unless we were going to the airport and she was saying goodbye. When she became a grandmother, she mellowed and started kissing the grandchildren and us once in a blue moon. My father was the same way. He never kissed or hugged us either. Maybe he learned from his parents (my paternal grandparents), as they never kissed us either. But we knew they really loved us but were not skillful enough to show emotions. My father and his parents cared about people of the world rather than their immediate family.

Mother had to work as a teacher in Reza Shah Kabir High School, and then she became the head of extracurricular activities. Her job would take her to the seaside for three months of the summer, as she was the head of camping for Tehran's high school students. My father claimed his blood pressure would drop if he would travel to the seaside and would stay home.

After their third divorce, the law would not let them remarry, so my father lives in Amirieh, in a building close to his brother, uncle Farrokh Zad, but in different levels in a high-rise. I went there a couple of times, and his house was small, with two rooms and a bathroom. He had a doll dressed like a Spanish girl and a drinking tray shaped as a car. Alcohol, which was hated by my mother and all of us, ruined his life.

When we were younger, my father lived with us at the big house in Darrous, north of Tehran. He taught me how to swim, and I remember I was looking at his back and thinking how white his skin was. He loved me and would let me read his translations, as he was fluent in English and would translate stories from *Reader's Digest*. He was very clever and had an above average IQ, like my aunt, his sister.

My father wrote poetry for my mother when they were dating or at the beginning of their marriage. If you would connect the first verse of each poem, you would either get my mother's first and last name or my mother's first, middle, and last name. That was what my mother wrote about the poems. But I noticed later that, if you connect the beginning and end of each section of each verse, her name would be spelled out—something my mother never noticed or appreciated. She was matter-of-fact, and he was in a world of poetry and politics. In every area, they were different—politics, poetry, music, you name it—but they loved each other. Go figure.

When, in the end, my father had a stroke and was in a coma for a year or so until he died, my mother was there every day taking care of him, though they were legally divorced. She never dated or married another guy, and he never remarried either.

In this process, only the children got hurt. That is why as soon as I realized that my son's father and I would start having arguments, I ended things. I did not at all want my son to see those days. I thought I was doing my son a favor by divorcing his father before we turned into my parents. So many times as I was crying under a blanket, I wished my parents would leave each other alone and go marry other people.

Mother managed to get her bachelor's degree in nutrition from *Madresse Aali Dokhtaran* to bring more money into the house, as father left after their first divorce. Also, she worked a double shift, one in the school and one in the Stadium Soraya, being in charge of the cafeteria. None of my friends knew how miserable our life was, as we lived in a big nice house in the north of Iran. And my aunt becoming famous, first as a member of parliament and then as deputy to the minister of education and next as the first woman to become minister of education did not help to make the world understand that we were not rich or happy. Now people really thought we had a wonderful life, carrying my aunt's last name and living next door to her and her family.

My aunt and cousins' house was our haven, since my aunt and her husband never quarreled. I even ran away from our house to my grandmother's house—from the northern part of Tehran to the southern part. What could a child do to show how much she was hurt? Later on, I did not wish that life for my son ever. Okay, as you see, there is a lot more to be written –the days of the revolution and all—but that is how I saw my personal life.

My father was only twenty years old and in the first year of studying law at his university when he fell in love with my mother, head to toe. He even ran away to Mashad, a city in the north of Iran, and confronted his friend Mr. Mehrpour, who would later become the head of extracurricular activities. He hid in Mr. Mehrpour's house writing poetry for my mother and complained, "They will not give their daughter to me." Mother was only sixteen.

He later became a judge (or prosecutor) but never really worked, as he was totally against the system. I am told by my cousins not to write that he was pro-Mosaddegh and not even to write a book. How rude, controlling, and undemocratic my cousins are. One day, they will understand. At any rate, he was so anti-regime that he would do anything to show his objection. He would never pay his traffic tickets, would drop the signs, and wrote poetry against the regime and pro-Mosaddegh. He loved Takhti, the wrestling hero and pro-National Front (Jebheh Melli) and even named my brother Mosaddegh. Not that it was right to do all of that, but he was thinking more of the Mass, Khalgh, than of his own little family.

My father had a broader vision, like Ghasem, the guy I fell in love with but who was killed in the revolution. And he never had a happy life. Only once after the revolution did I ask him, "Father, which political group do you agree with?"

And he said, "Nehzat Azadi," meaning the new version of National Front, a pro-Mosaddegh group with Dr. Bazargan as the leader of that party at the time of the revolution and the prime minister after the revolution. Later on, when the revolution changed its face to a total religious face (my father hated religion), he had the shock of his life.

I was in the United States, in Virginia, when he died.

Father's death, 1991

The first time I noticed something was wrong was when there was a party and a family gathering at the house of Maliheh, a cousin in Maryland. I noticed that, every time I walked in the big party room, everybody would get quiet. It bothered me so much that I spent the whole time in a little room adjacent to the big living room. They all knew that my father had had a stroke and was in a coma, except me. My sister made sure no one would tell me so I would not travel to Iran. She feared two things—first, that I, being against the regime after the revolution, would be rearrested by the guards and, second, that I would confront her no-good husband over what he had done to me in Germany. I found out months later that my father was in coma.

My friend, Tye, came to the Washington/Virginia area to visit her daughter and me. We went to a Persian restaurant to have Persian food. Then I had to drive her to the airport. As we were sitting in the restaurant, the people next to us said, "Ooh, they just bombarded the hospital in Tehran." It was the same hospital my father was in. I collapsed. I couldn't drive my friend to the airport, and she had to drive my car. I was so sad and angry.

I heard later that my mother had pushed a wheelchair with my father in it to safe place in the hospital, as it was bombarded by Iraqis.

It was close to the new year. I called Iran, and the no-good husband of my sister picked up the phone, as the rest were at the hospital. He started passing his dirty comments at me and telling me, "Can I love you in my heart? I need to!"

I was furious. First, what terrible timing. Second, the harassment was continuing and now verbally. Third, why would you need my approval for your dirty mind?

I went to California that year for the Persian New Year, and I wore my new white dress. My brother from San Diego arrived, and we all gathered around the Norooz celebration table at my cousin Nahid's house. Right after Persian New Year started, we heard that our father died. The busiest time to call Tehran is right at Persian New Year. I immediately tried and tried to call Tehran. The news was confirmed by Kourosh, my cousin in Tehran.

My brother Farhad and I went to a small room and just sat there in sorrow. Relatives showed up and took us out of the room. I changed my clothes to black. I felt like I'd just hit a wall. I had lots of unfinished business with my father. We were all waiting for a peaceful day. With his death, another reality hit me—that there would never be a good resolution between my parents. I heard my mother took care of him in his last days better that any wife could. Some strange love they had for each other.

Every Norooz I have to think of him and I have to celebrate the New Year and then, in hiding, cry for him. He had a very clever brain, and it was a waste for it to be buried under dirt in a grave. I wish a brain transplant had been invented. It hasn't been invented yet, but maybe when my grandchildren have their kids and read this, they may say, "Oh, it's here now" (like phones and cell phones).

CHAPTER 26

MY FORMER MOTHER- AND FATHER-IN-LAW

Touri Joon and Baba Joon, the way my son calls them, are my son's paternal grandparents. Touran Parvin Eshgh Abadi is her full name. Asasadollah Sanii, former Rashidi, is his full name. My former father-in-law and grandpa of my son was secretary of defense, deputy to Mosaddegh, secretary of agriculture, and head of a branch of the oil company in Iran. He was a Baha'i who was rejected by fate, as the Baha'i are forbidden to interfere in politics. But he was an exception and actually the Baha'i loved him. I can not tell their story without jumping years back and also years forward. So please bear with me.

At one point, I was talking almost daily to Touri Joon. I was selling my house in Monterey around 2015, waiting for the paperwork and packing all my stuff. I had enough time on my hand. I saw that I had a piece of art from my three uncles, even the one who was not an artist but a physician; from my cousin Shirin, who is "the artist" in my eyes; and from Sepideh, my sister's daughter but none from Bahman's mother. She was an artist in my eyes, and she was a beautiful painter. Her teacher was Katoozian, a true artist in my eyes.

As we were talking in 2014 or 2015, our conversation developed to her telling me her life story. When I was young and just married, I would hardly talk to my parents-in-law more than necessary—like my daughter-in-law and me in a way. This time, we were talking like two mature people. I even recorded some of her words. She told me how she made her own dress to go to the wedding of the Shah and his second wife, Queen Soraya; how she took the general, her husband, to a dermatologist for his back spots; and how she considered herself pro-Bakhtiary or

Ghashghaee tribe. I bought one of her paintings of some yellow roses and another with some women villagers walking in a forest. She told me how her grandpa or maybe her father was a tea merchant who came from Eshgh Abbad, a city in Russia, to Iran. And she talked about how being Baha'i was difficult. She told how Mahvi, her uncle and a good friend of the Shah, was once arrested and in the desert, the Bakhtiaris or Ghasghaees (I don't remember which) came to his rescue.

I have about three tapes of these conversations with her. But as she was saying, "Don't record me," and knew I was recording, she told me a lot. A lifetime of talking happened, and maybe one day I will translate those conversations. She lived with her mother-in-law and sisters-in-laws when she first got married. But they lived on a separate floor altogether, while I had lived in a basement with no kitchen and years and years later. I just thanked her for taking care of my son. She is now in special housing, as she had developed Alzheimer amnesia lately. I am glad I have her words.

As for General Sanii, he was from Hamadan, a city in Iran that, during King Dariush's time, was the capital. He knew how to speak Turkish, but he looked a lot like Brezhnev, a Russian politician and president. The eyebrows were the same and the chin maybe. He always reminded me of that Russian president. He was, at one point, working with Reza Shah the father. Then he served as deputy to Mosaddegh and again as a devoted general and secretary of war in Shah Mohammad Reza Shah's regime. He had lots of history of Iran in his heart. But when I once asked him to write his memoires, he said, "So far, whoever has written his memoires is regretting it." He was just happy to be alive and out of reach of the fake religious regime in Iran. As a military man in the Shah's time and a Baha'i, he was in double danger.

I saw him a lot in Geneva and once in Vancouver. He died and was buried in Vancouver in 1997. He had a lot to say and experienced different eras. I am sure he suffered as a Baha'i. In my mind, women are suffering double in Iran, as they live in a dictatorship and are mandated to wear hijabs. Everybody suffered in this regime after the revolution in one way or the other.

I was reading the first pages of a book written by General Sanii called *Yadha va*

Yaddashtha (*Memories and Memoires*). He writes how, after he was in prison and then released after six months, in 1980, the guards of Khomeini entered his house and confiscated everything. They did the same thing at my aunt's house. They take your most personal things away. He says in that book he had two choices—to commit suicide in order not to bother anyone around him or to run away. So he decided to run away to Turkey with a fake passport for him and a true passport for his brother who'd bailed him out of prison. I hope someone translates that book, since, after the revolution, anytime I saw him, he was just writing and writing—though not as a book but as a therapy and to record scattered memories. He was born in the dynasty of Ghajars and lived thru the Reza Shah and Mohammad Reza Shah eras and had a lot to say.

Here I must mention a Baha'i woman who is my hero. Tahereh Ghoratol Ain (or just Tahereh) is one of my idols. She was a Baha'i/ Bábí woman. Her name means "the Pure One," and her title means "Solace/Consolation of the Eyes." She was born in 1817 and executed somewhere between August 16 and 27, 1852). An influential poet, women's right activist, and theologian, Tahereh was killed by fundamentalists for the brave act of unveiling—buried alive in a wall. Here is a short description of her heroic act:

> Táhirih was probably best remembered for unveiling herself in an assemblage of men during the Conference of Badasht. The unveiling caused a great deal of controversy and the Báb named her "the Pure One" to show his support for her. She was soon arrested and placed under house arrest in Tehran. In mid-1852, she was executed in secret on account of her Bábí faith and her unveiling. Before her death, she declared, "You can kill me as soon as you like, but you cannot stop the emancipation of women." Since her death, Bábí and Baha'i literature venerated her to the level of martyr, being described as "the first woman suffrage martyr."

She is my model. If all women of the world had her bravery, we would not have mandatory hijabs anywhere, especially in Iran. And for that matter we need brave men too.

I hope by the time I finish this book, or by the time I can still travel, I will be able to take my son to visit Iran. He was born there but has never seen it, just as I was born in Abadan and have never seen it. Life has its own games to play with us.

CHAPTER 27

MY PATERNAL GRANDPARENTS

My father's parents were pioneers in their time. My grandpa, who we called Agha Joon, was named Farrokh Din Parsay. His last name was formerly Naraghee. He was a journalist and also anti-religion to the core. Sometime in his family's life, all their birth certificates were changed, and he chose for most of the names of his family members to start with Farrokh; God knows why. Farrokh means "happy" or "delightful." He also added the month that the children were born to their names. My aunts and uncles names, and especially my grandma's, are all difficult to remember. We children used to make fun of their names and say, "If we have a soar throat, we can't call grandma Fakhr Afagh, meaning "the honor of the world." Their children's names are Farvardin, my eldest uncle; Esfand Madoveh Farrokh Rou; Farrokh Zaman; Azar Madoveh Farrokh Zad; and Aban Madoveh Farookh Pour. Madoveh means "was invited to this world." I bet you my grandpa was reading books with a lot of Arabic names, since Arabic is mixed with Farsi a lot, and all great poems of Iran did recite poetry in both languages. Well the question would be, If you chose the last name to be Parsay coming from Pars and totally Persian, then why did all the first names have some Arabic in them?

My grandpa's room in the upstairs part of our house, which was a separate level, was full of newspapers. *Ettelaat, Khandaniha, SepidoSiah,* were the four media sources in Iran at that time, and he had volumes of each stacked up to the ceiling. He should be thankful that he did not have allergy to paper, ink, or dust. I very rarely went to his room, and if he was home, he would be writing. He was humorous, as were all his children, including my father. He would make alcohol out of sour cherries and sometimes talk about China and Mao. That said, he did not like us as much he did my aunt's children in the house next door. Up to this day, we don't know why, and my other cousin, Saideh, feels the same.

I found out about his death while studying at Purdue. He had heart problems, but even under strict rest orders from doctors, would ask to have lottery tickets bought for him.

It was 1971, and I walked into the library of Purdue University. Newspapers were hanging from long sticks, including *Ettelaat* or *Keyhan*, two famous newspapers from Iran. Iranian students would go and read them. As I opened the newspaper, I saw a part of it had been cut with scissors. I wondered what the news was. At that time, calling Iran was not easy, and there were no text messages. So you had to wait till the next aerogram letter, which was on special blue paper, to arrive from Iran. I got the news of his death and cried, though I thought I did not have great memories of him. I found out that one of the students had done the cutting so I would not read the news and get a shock. I found out later that my grandpa had written not to hold any ceremonies out of sadness for him and to treat him like all humans, who are condemned to die one day. He was praised by that paper.

My grandpa owned a newspaper called *Asre Ahan* (*The Iron Century*). He also put his name on my grandma's paper, called *Jahan Zanan* (*The World of Women*). He was a man who did a lot for the women's movement. At that time, the name of a woman could not be listed as owner of a paper. (It was 1919. In the United States, in 1920, women got the right to vote.) He paid heavily for that, as he was threatened accused of being a Baha'i, and had to change jobs and locations a lot—sometimes by order of the government and sometimes for safety. They were also exiled to a small city.

What I regret is that I never sat him and my grandma down to have them tell us their memories. What we saw was not what they really were. I do encourage my son and his children to do that. Grandmas have a lot to share—from their grandparents time up through the time of their children's marriage. From then on, one's spouse and his or her parents share memories together. But a lot happens in the family before that time and needs to be told. I do my best by writing this book.

My grandmother, who we called Mamane Bala, meaning "the grandma upstairs," not to be mixed with the other grandma, was called Fakhr Afagh Parsay. Her name used to be Batoul before being changed. She was also married before she married my grandfather and had a son called Rouh Allah, meaning "the spirit of God." Her first husband's last name was Javadi. Her room was simple—two rooms really, one with her bed and an extra bed that the grandchildren would sleep in when they stayed with her. She had a TV and one picture on the mantle of she and the king's twin sister, Ashraf, and two other women. To us, they were friends, but she was granted some prizes for being a pioneer in women's suffrage, and her picture was somewhere in the parliament, Mjlis. The other two women, one of whom had big lips to me, were pioneers too. Stupid us, we never asked her who they were, and she never volunteered to give me any information. It was a torture for us grandkids when it became our turn to sleep in her room because she could not hear properly due to old age. Her TV was loud, and the clock on the wall would sound loudly too. She would complain of rheumatic and arthritic pain in her lumbar, and we had to listen to that. Next to her bed were two books. One was a direct method to teach you English, and the other was an English-Farsi dictionary. I always wondered why she was learning a new language when she was in contact with no one. She was a pioneer in everything she did. She would only cook a dish called *dampokhtak*, a yellow rice and dried fava beans.

When I returned from the United States, which was after the death of my grandpa, she had moved to my aunt's house, and my mother bought the whole house and remodeled it. She was on a strict diet and could not move around. And the various facilities that a house assist older people today did not exist then. I have a clinch in my heart when I see those devices that enable you to sit on a chair and be taken upstairs and downstairs. My grandma lived on the top floor of my aunt's forever, except when a reporter would come to interview her. She was sitting in that room when the revolutionary guards in Iran moved my aunt to the prison, and she saw that. She hit her chest so hard that she died days after in my uncle Farrokh Zad's house.

The sad part of it was that, all her life, she'd made sure that everyone knew that her *kafan* (the cloth, or shroud, Muslims and Jews are buried in) was under her bed.

She asked everyone to bury her in that special kafan. In the end the most intellectual among us are superstitious. But when all that happened and she was rushed to my uncle Farrokh Zad's house, no one was thinking of that.

At her burial, instead of her son-in-law, who would normally go in the grave and pray for her, my cousin Saeed did that, due to the fact that General Shirin Sokhan (her son-in-law) was in the prison with my aunt. After the ceremony was finished, I saw Susan, my cousin, running with the Kafan in her hands shouting, "Wait, wait, but I have the Kafan." But the ceremony was finished, and she was buried.

I got a good look at her face. She was very much at peace, as if she was resting and taking a nap. She did not see how the regime killed her daughter, how all her fights for freedom of women went to waste, or how the whole country went backward. She was lucky in that way. May she rest in peace. She was a true pioneer for women. She is buried in Beheshte Zahra cemetery close to her husband, my grandpa, who died when I was studying at Purdue. So much happened after that.

CHAPTER 28

IRAN–IRAQ WAR, 1980–1988

Right after my divorce from Bahman, I moved to my mother's house in Gheytarieh. My father was living in Amirieh due to their third divorce but would visit often. I heard that, the day after I left, Bahman and his family enrolled my son in kindergarten. They never gave me its address, maybe thinking I would kidnap him. I was trying to protect him, thinking, first, that not being in a household with too many arguments and quarrels between his parents was good for him and, second, that being a Baha'i descendant was dangerous for him.

After all it is still unsafe for the Baha'i more than for others in 2020. Iran is not even safe for humankind at the moment. As I write these words, the Corona virus is spreading all over, and the government of Iran is not considerate of its people. In addition, Baha'is can't study or work there.

At that time when I was twenty-seven years old and getting a divorce, I was not skillful enough to know that, for my son, being with his mother was important too. But again, a sad and angry mother leads to an angry household. And with my childhood experience and my parents divorces, I thought I was buying him safety and happiness. I did not know that, by that separation, I was stabbing my heart, with an instrument that remains still. And every time I see my son, which isn't often, it's like someone is turning the knife in my heart. I don't know how to ask him for forgiveness for my ignorance.

In a short while, Bahman's family left for England. Meanwhile, for a period of six months, Bahman's father, General Sanii, was imprisoned, and he worked in the prison's kitchen. After a short while, Bahman and Babak, my son, left Iran for England and waited for their immigration papers to arrive from Canada. His mother and sister and aunt left via donkeys at night to Turkey. His father and uncle left in a car and were smuggled through the Turkish border. Then all of them, plus my son, went to Geneva, Switzerland.

I will get to that part, but a lot happened then. I may forget the sequence of events, but I know that, once the government announced that those who had two houses under their name had to give one to the government. It happened that both my mother and sister were abroad, and only my father and I were in Iran at the time. So I got power of attorney from both my sister and my mother. Then I put my mother's apartment in Farmanieh in my sister Shahla's name. I went to the Registration of Legal Affairs office. Some mullahs were there, and one took my case. He started opening his desk drawers, and I am looking around, not knowing what to do. I left and called my father from a public phone, something that does not exist nowadays due to the advent of cell phones. My father joined me, and we both went back to the office. He paid the bribe and very angrily said, "Don't ever call me for these matters." He was against corruption and bribery but was forced to do it to rescue the house.

We did a lot out of fear of the new regime—burning pictures, hiding books, and all. I also called Tichner, the foreign student advisor of Purdue, and asked Nona, the secretary, for a fake I-20 for my brother to leave Iran. Although it took us a lot of efforts to bring him over, since he walked in with a guitar and all music instruments were banned, we immediately figured that he should leave Iran ASAP.

CHAPTER 29

LEAVING IRAN FOR SWITZERLAND, 1981

Remember what happened in Berlin? Now the news came that my sister's husband was returning to Iran. I had to change plans and leave Iran quickly with no money and no job, instead of waiting till Bahman and Babak got to Canada. I hated him that much and did not want to see him unless I was forced to. I took the leap in the dark, and the anticipation of seeing my child again was helping me to move faster. My sister's husband was arriving at night, and I managed to leave at noon. The least I could do was not give him the satisfaction of seeing me again—not wait for an opportunity for him to torture me more verbally by flirting.

I did not have enough money to manage changing countries, but I did it anyway. Hope was all I had. A woman can be a stripper or a model or in contact with a hundred men and sleeping with half of them. But when one she does not want to sleep with takes advantage of a situation and circumstances and sleeps with her, it's a rape in any woman's book. Like Weinstein, he is a rapist to me forever and more.

But now I was leaving Iran for Switzerland in the middle of the Iran-Iraq War. The night before I left Iran, I got a call from an anonymous person. He threatened me, saying that he was calling from the passport department. He said, you, the Baha'i. We won't let you leave Iran. I got scared. My father was calm and said, "Don't worry."

I said, "I'll go and spend the night at my friend Nasi's house."

I asked Mansoor, my friend and my uncle's friend, to come to the airport with me. He knew how to handle those guards. He also taught me to drop my wedding ring at the last moment after they checked my suitcase, while I was closing the zipper. My suitcase was not locked, and the most valuable thing I had was in it. I did that since it was totally forbidden to take any jewelry out of Iran. In addition, you were allowed to leave with only a limited amount of money. These women with long black covers, none of whom looked like my countrymen, searched my body in a very bad manner. They were impolite to us on purpose. I hugged Mansoor and thanked him.

We flew to Switzerland, and I could not wait to get my suitcase. I went to a hotel and dropped the suitcase on my bed and searched inside it with my fingers to touch the ring. It was there. Thank God. All the money I had to my name consisted of a few dollars, four gold bracelets, a pearl necklace, and my maternal grandma's diamond ring that was given to me when I gave birth to Babak. I had a visa for three months only and no job. The future was dark, but I was extremely happy because I could see my dear son after so long.

I found a place called Foyer L'Accuel ran by French nuns. We each had a room with a bed and a small sink. The bathrooms and showers were shared on each floor. It was like a dormitory again. The nuns would serve us rabbits on Sunday, and I could not eat that. I met Shahla, Shahnaz, and Behnaz, three Iranian girls. After the revolution, finding Iranians everywhere was easy, as many left that crazy country. My friendship with Shahnaz continued until later in life for a while.

Shahla had a friend called Linus, who was the grandchild of Dr. Linus Pauling who discovered that vitamin C is good for colds and got a Nobel Prize for it. They were millionaires. Shahla was invited there one day, and she took me with her. Linus liked me, and I told him my story. He said he would invite me to Switzerland for three more months until I found a job and got a Carte de Sejour, the equivalent of a green card in the United States.

As we were sitting next to his pool at his house, I said, "I don't know if I can pay for my next month's rent, and I may have to sell my gold bracelets."

He sympathized with me and said, "Yes, this year we've had to watch our budget too. We decided not to warm up the pool's water."

I looked at him with my mouth open. I realized how, when I was richer than some, some of my comments must have been a shock to some. How far apart are these two worlds—that of the rich and that of the poor. Revolution teaches you quickly.

I took Linus Pauling's invitation letter to the embassy, got a lawyer called Mlle Bertchi, and got my permit to work and live temporarily in Switzerland. Now I had to find a job right away.

Picture 12 from left to right / top to bottom

- Servants as relatives with brothers and Hasan and firoozeh children who used to be queen Farah's servant at her childhood
- Vajieh and her husband and children lived with us at the end of this yard
- Nejati my cousin's next door driver, I drove with sometimes, and the special driver of my aunt when she was the Secretary of Education Mr. Rezaee.
- Pari and Mehri children of khaleh Shokat who was like relatives of my mother
- Naneh this Iraqi woman that always lived with my aunt family next door

Picture 13 from left to right / top to bottom

- Purdue 1972 with Ghasem
- Purdue end of 1972 Ghasem, me, Marmar, Susan, Majid
- Purdue Same party with Kerry (Bahman's girl friend), Bahman, Reza, me,
- Hamid my cousin and I at soccer game in Purdue
- Bahman's house Purdue, my birthday 1973
- Birthday party Bahman threw for me, guests were singing wedding songs

Picture 14 from left to right / top to bottom

- My wedding with mother, guest, me, maternal grandma Zinat Joon
- Wedding day the one on far left is khaleh Victor as Bahman's aunt
- My aunt (Dr. Parsay), Bahman, me, Touran Sanii Bahman's mother
- My aunt (Secretary of Education at the time and relatives witnessing my marriage to Bahman)

Picture 15 from left to right / top to bottom

- Babak my son at the day of his Valimeh like christening Baha'i Style
- With Babak at Bahman's parent house
- Being pregnant with my son Babak with sister's daughter and brother

- Being nine months pregnant with Babak at General Sanii's house
- Babak few months old in San Francisco

Picture 16 from left to right / top to bottom

- Visiting Babak in Seattle after years before getting my green card
- Visiting Babak my son in Tehran, revolution time
- Lost all my pictures of Switzerland, this is with borrowed friends in VA
- Another year Babak Visitations in my Alexandria VA house balcony
- Babak my son with Yazdan a very kind and good hearted relative in Canada
- One of Babak's visits in Baltimore at the age of 13 with a friend

Picture 17 from left to right / top to bottom

- • Every year that my son visited me from 4 to 6 days I would take him to Sears and take a picture with him and live with that picture until the next year

Picture 18 from left to right / top to bottom

- The only picture Babak has with my father since a lot got lost in revolution
- At airport my son's departure after one of the yearly visitation
- Babak With a friend and my mother in Alexandria Va
- With Babak my son he is showing off his watch
- At Vancouver with Babak at a relative's house going to see a lawyer
- Mother after her operation and Babak and me Persuan new year Va

Picture 19 from left to right / top to bottom

- My aunt Dr.Farrokh Rou Parsay we called her ammeh joon, in Shah's cabinet
- My aunts handwriting a page of her Memoire in Farsi
- Me and my cousins at my aunts grave a year after her execution by regime
- Guessing my aunts grave after it was demolished by the regime a few times
- My wedding night with Mrs Sanii, 2 guests, me Bahman and my aunt Dr. Parsay

Picture 20 from left to right / top to bottom

- With a coworker and Dick Holmberg doing IDMS and COBOL programming
- In Switzerland one of my jobs as computer programmer
- As a salesman in Garfinkel clothing store
- At a 2K job contractor to convert dates in computers to 2000
- Teaching Farsi in VA
- As a Computer Programmer in Greenville S Carolina

Picture 21 from left to right / top to bottom

- My IDs at Purdue and different jobs and some very good people in my life
- Shahram my cousin and his family and Claudia his wife who I lived with in CA
- Mani and Afsaneh as groom and bride who helped me during my life
- Mary my best friend who saved my furniture and life

Picture 22 from left to right / top to bottom

- Grave of my mother that I have never seen in person
- Grave of my Grandma that I have never seen in person and is demolished now
- Grave of my father that I visited on my last trip to Iran 1992

Picture 23 from left to right / top to bottom

- My political pictures giving flowers to the King Mohammad Reza Shah
- With Dr. & Mrs. Matin Daftari head of National front & Mosadegh Grandchild
- With the singer Marzieh that joined Mojahedin of Iran
- With Shahnaz that introduces me to leftist and Cheriks in DC
- In Paris with Mr. Rezae of NCR

Picture 24 from left to right / top to bottom

- My sister Shahla's wedding to Mehrdad Seifollahi when I was in America
- My marriage with Bahman in the same room in our house
- Moe & me & a friend, Mamad taught me the philosophy of the leftists
- Second marriage to Farrokh to free him from Iran Iraq war & get him a Visa
- Last marriage to Mehrdad Saba for a year, in Cancun
- With Daria and his nice sister and children at my last trip to Iran 1992

Picture 25 from left to right / top to bottom

- Babak's marriage to Claudia at SF City Hall with family and friends 2008
- Babak my son getting his Phd from UC Davis with me and Claudia
- Babak getting his degree from Cornell University

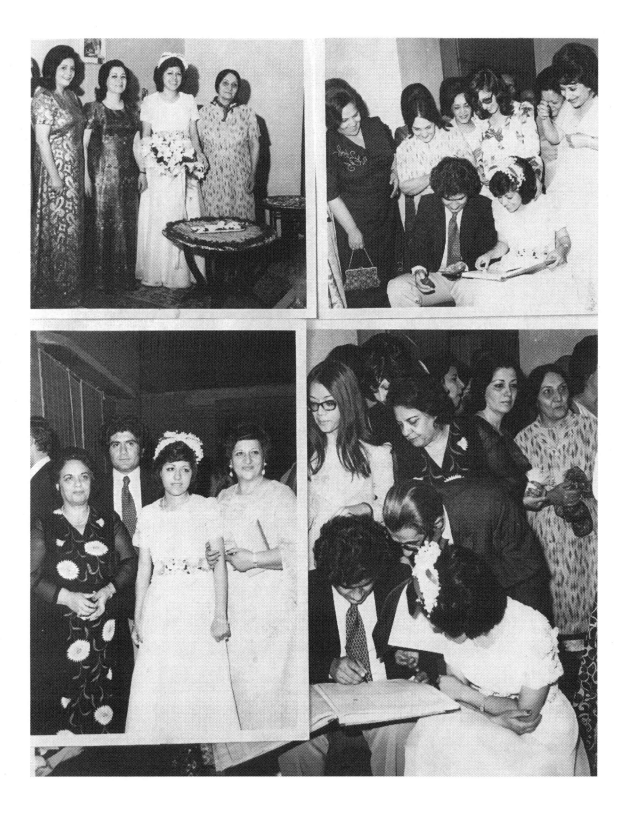

Saturday ۹–۳۵۶ شنبه

12 MARCH 1977	۲۱ اسفند ۱۳۵۵	۲۱ ربیع‌الاول ۱۳۹۷
3	۱۲	۳

ساعت

Am.

۷ ...

۸ ...

۹ ...

۱۰ ...

۱۱ ...

۱۲ ...

۱۳ ...

۱۴ ...

۱۵ ...

۱۶ ...

۱۷ ...

۱۸ ...

۱۹ ...

۲۰ ...

۲۱ ...

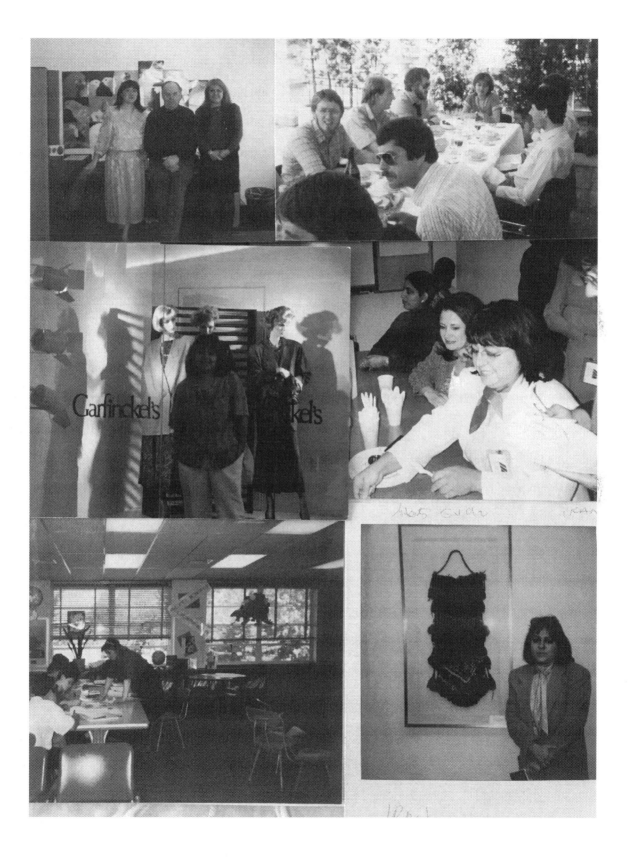

CHAPTER 30

SEEING MY CHILD AGAIN IN SWITZERLAND, 1981–1983

At last the day came that I could see my son. I went to Bahman's family's apartment in a beautiful part of Geneva, and usually whatever house they had abroad was under the name of Jaleh. My heart was in my mouth, beating rapidly. I was thinking, *What does he look like now? Will he recognize me? What does he like or dislike?*

I knocked at the door, and the door opened. I could not see who opened the door. My eyes were wandering around the house to find my son. I said hello quickly and entered and called, "Babak Joon."

A little boy ran fast and hid behind a couch.

I said "Babak Joon?" and ran toward him.

He ran away. I had to run around the room and next to the bedroom to catch him. He did not want to see me. How sad. He was hurt or maybe he'd heard much bad stuff about me. I don't know. But I had to hold him tightly so he would not run away. I kissed him and kissed him, and he was hesitant until he got calmer. I looked at him and cried. I loved him so much and did not know what to do or say.

Then we all sat down and caught up on the news. I knew they were on their way to Canada. I asked them if I could come and visit him for as long as they were in Switzerland. I wanted to go swimming with him, since they had an indoor pool in that apartment complex in Geneva. I wanted to be there every night—to give him a bath and tell him stories. I wanted him, in his little mind, to find out that I loved him and that I would tell him my side of the story when he grew older.

One day, as I was drying his hair after a bath, suddenly the hair dryer in my hand caught fire. He ran away, and I dropped the hairdryer. I was not allowed to do that anymore. Another day, I was telling him a story before he went to bed and it was about a dragon that came to town and had fire coming out of his mouth, and the hero killed him. The next day, they said, "Don't tell him bedtime stories." I was to leave right before he went to bed. The reason was that he'd started crying and saying, "What if the fire went to the other levels of that building and the whole house was set on fire?" My luck.

During one of my visits I told my former in-laws that I was looking for a job. Bahman said his mother's uncle, Mr. Mahvi, who was a successful businessman and a friend of the Shah, had a business in Geneva. I said I know computers; maybe he would hire me. Bahman arranged an interview with him. I took my documents and degrees and all and had an interview with him, and he liked me.

The next day, I saw that Bahman's mother had gotten dressed up. She said she was going to see Mahvi. They were close friends, since her mother had raised Mahvi. He was the favorite uncle of the mother. After that, I got news that Mahdi was not going to hire me. I was very hurt and cried dearly; if I did not find a job, I would have to leave and go back to Iran. Bahman still liked me, and I had to be very nice to him to see my son. But I was puzzled—no money, no job.

That was when I applied to a Greek company, where English was spoken. My job search was limited to companies where English was spoken, as my French at that time consisted of only "madam," "monsieur," and "merci." If someone had asked me, "Parle vous angles?" I would not have understood that they are asking me, "Do you speak English?"

But I was learning rapidly and soon was able to go to the market and buy a car and get insurance for it. Those who lived in Switzerland know that people and bus drivers and shop owners speak French, Italian, and German and totally refuse to switch to English. At that age, I had to learn a new language and quickly.

I got hired by this Greek company and learned a little Greek too. A Canadian was my coworker, and I could speak English to him. A guy called Yani would come from Greece, and one day, we went to lunch. He was trying to tell me he was gay. He pointed to a girl coming toward us and she was pretty and walking sexy. He asked me, "Do you feel anything special when you see her?"

I said, "No. Why?"

He said, "Me neither. But if he walks that way"—he pointed to a guy—"I feel something in my heart." He also said, "My mother is praying and waiting for me to invite a girl to our pool party at home," adding, "It will not happen."

I said, "Pity," because he was very good-looking and handsome, as most gay men are.

When I entered Bahman's parents' house for the first time to see Babak, I noticed there was a couple living there too. Bahman's mother's sister married Bahman's father's brother. We called them Khaleh Victor and Amoo Parviz. I could not be happier for Babak having these kind people around him too. The reason they were there too was that Amoo Parviz was the bail (*zamen*) for Timsar Sanii when he was in jail. When he left the country illegally, his brother and his family were supposed to leave too, as they would be arrested by the guards of the revolution in Iran. They shared a bedroom in that house.

We played a card game called Belot—Tour Joon, Bahman's mother; Amoo Parviz, Bahman's father's brother; Khaleh Victor, his wife; Touri Joon's sister; and me. It was the best hobby the four of us could have those days. Timsar would go for a walk, and we would play cards, or I would go swimming with Bahman and Babak. Life was happy—until Bahman brought this French girl home as his girlfriend.

I was not his wife and could not say anything, but I was sooo jealous, especially when she would play with Babak. I wanted to tell her to shut up. This is my son. Stay away. But if she were to marry Bahman, she would have more power over Babak.

In the end, Bahman did not marry her, but later, after they moved to Canada, he married a beautiful Baha'i Canadian girl called Natasha. She had a son from her previous marriage too, and they all lived in a house together. He divorced her after he had a son with her called Dara, my son's half brother. Later, he married an American Canadian called Terry, which whom he has a son called Chris. They all live in Canada.

I never had another child in my life, and at one point, I really wanted one. But God had other plans for me. We will get to that part.

For that period, I was happy seeing Babak. Once, when he was sick, the family made sure I saw him, and once we had that meeting at Bahman's sister Jaleh's house. My visits were always short.

Amoo and Khaleh Victor were applying for Canada too, and all of their papers arrived at the same time. I only know that, after they all left for Canada, I started living like a zombie. And whatever decision I made was wrong, especially with men. I felt a hole in my life that I thought I could temporarily soothe with a man in my life, a husband. But, no, this was a very temporary patch, and the void was greater than that.

I began living on survival mode.

CHAPTER 31

MY MOTHER IN CAPTIVITY OVER A VISA, 1983

Once during the hostage crisis, my mother decided to go to California to visit my brother and his wife. They advised her to go to Mexico and they would get a lawyer to bring her in. She went to a border city of Mexico and San Diego. The lawyer, or maybe a stupid friend, suggested that my mother could walk with a Mexican worker into the United States, and when she was inside, the lawyer would work on getting her a green card to stay.

At the border, the Mexican officers stopped my mother and asked for her papers. Now, many millions of Mexicans were, at that time, entering the United States illegally, and just my mother was arrested. She was tall and white. I don't know. Maybe she was smiling like she smiled in the Swiss embassy. So they arrested her and took her to a prison in Tijuana. I have the notebook that was her diary she wrote in almost every day while there. She gave it to me one day and said, "Write about it." She had this vision of me that either I would be a very important person or a great writer. I hope it comes true. In summary, she wrote, "It's so unsafe and depressing in this prison. All the people eat beans and smell. I see rats the size of raccoons. I asked the prison guard to give me a sewing machine so I could make clothes."

I remember when I was four and my sister was seven, Mother would, as usual, sew our clothes. My sister would cry that she did not want to look like me, so Mother had to remove the pretty pictures she'd put on the front of her clothes. She was using a hot iron, and I was wondering, *What is wrong with me that she so hates to look like me?* I had that picture too. My mother was a great cook and tailor and all. She was only too angry, bad tempered, and controlling. She was a great manager too, as she took three hundred or more students to the camp; managed the teachers and workers, mostly men beneath her; and was loved by all. For me. I was under her surveillance and had no privacy or power of decision making.

At any rate, she was released from that prison and was allowed to return to Iran but not to America. This is what she did, as she would listen to nobody when she had a plan in her mind. My mother went to Canada, and there, with the excuse of visiting my son, stayed there and got a lawyer and became a Canadian citizen for two years. My youngest brother joined her too.

But my mother, being impatient, decided to try going to the United States one more time. She flew to Switzerland, where I was residing at that time, and I took her to the American embassy in Bern. She got the visa. However, she lost her rights to become a citizen of Canada. This was characteristic of her. She would get bored and impatient very quickly.

My cousin Mahshid said that, once, my mother went to her house to visit her. As soon as she opened the door and my mother entered her house, she said, "Okay. I saw you, and you are okay. Now I have to leave."

My cousin said, "Wow Shokouh Joon" (meaning dear Shokouh; in Farsi, *joon* is attached to any name as dear; I call my son Babak Joon) "you have not even entered the house. Just come in, and let's have a cup of tea together."

My mother said, "No. I just wanted to make sure that you are okay. And now I have to go."

She was restless everywhere. In each country, she would miss the other child and/or want to return to Iran. But among her good character traits were here persistence and diligence. She had a daughter in Switzerland, and one in Iran, as well as a son in Canada and a son in the United States. She did not know who to attend to, and she wanted them all, as her whole life was devoted to "these four"—words we heard a million times in our lifetime. "If it were not for these four," she would say, meaning her kids, meaning us. I felt a lot of pressure for having been born and giving her so much trouble.

When I got older and learned some psychology, I understood her character better, but it was too late. I was an angry person. My youngest brother is a very angry person. And we have a right to be. I am working on myself, though, and maybe he is too. But for us, separation and not talking to each other became a norm—as we saw how our parents would separate and then get back together. We thought this was what loving meant, cycles of separation and togetherness. Normal families looked weird to me when they showed too much love toward each other. Just as my relation with my son is weird and not normal, so were my relationships with my parents and sister and brothers.

My mother would visit me on any occasion—in Switzerland; in Indiana; in Washington, DC.

After a while, my mother came to Geneva to visit me and apply for a visa for the United States. By that time, she had gone from Mexico to Canada and now was in Switzerland on her way back to Iran. But her trip was not finished. She was about to go back to the United States. She said her uncle, Agha Daee Ghasem, would recite a proverb that said, "Stone is free; sparrow is free." It meant, give it a try and see if you can get a visa there.

I took her to the American embassy in Bern, the capital of Switzerland. We took a train, and it was during the hostage taking in Iran. We had to hide our identities as Iranian.

Once in a train, I lied and said, "I am from Spain."

The Swiss people know lots of languages, so the guy started speaking Spanish to me.

I smiled and said, "Oh, I was a little girl when I left there and don't know the language."

From then on, I stopped lying but, rather, changed the subject. As soon as people knew we were Iranians, they would stop talking to us. The government of Iran at that time was the weirdest government on earth. Though it was anti-humanity and anti-religion, the regime called itself a republic and Islamic—two giant lies.

At any rate, my mother and I went to the embassy, and since my mother didn't know English, she was forcing a smile the whole time. Surprisingly, the ambassador gave her a visa. I noticed my mother was not excited. We thanked them and left the office.

Outside I asked, "How come you are not excited?"

She said, "Why should I be? We did not get the visa."

I said, "What do you mean? You did get the visa." I had forgotten to translate that part.

She screamed and was very happy. She left for the United States, and I was alone again.

CHAPTER 32

RESCUING ONE PERSON FROM THE WAR, 1983

After Babak and Bahman and his family left for Canada, I continued living in my studio in Meyrin at the border of France. I would go shopping for wine and water and meat in France and would come back to Geneva and my studio in Meyrin. In France, even the table wine was delicious, unlike in California. Everything tasted better in Europe and even better in Iran. Maybe that was due to freshness, less hormones, and nothing frozen at that time. Chocolate croissants were my favorite.

Yani told me there was a good opportunity in the branch of the digital computer company in Geneva. I applied and was accepted. Purdue University graduates were always chosen by job givers. Bahman used to say, "How come you are successful at work and know what to do? Apply the same to your personal life."

I liked the digital company for two reasons. First, I had some idea of its computer system, since we'd used digital computers when I'd worked for the court affairs office in Iran. Second, it was forbidden to speak any language except English; that was a big plus for me. My manager was a guy from New Zealand. He had red hair and was very meticulous. We would have meetings, and he would remind me of Popeye the Sailor Man. I don't know why.

Mlle Bertchi gave me my green card equivalent, which allowed me to stay and work in Switzerland. Linie was traveling a lot, and I was lonely. I thought that, before my grandma died I had to go to Iran for a short visit and see her. The first time I traveled to Iran, I was thinking that I should marry. First, that would ensure that my sister's no-good husband would stay away from me as a married woman. And maybe I could have a child, and this child would be totally mine. I was that stupid and out of this world. Again, you want logic? Go read a fiction. This is the real biography of my life. In addition, neither my mother nor sister believed me.

The relative of my brother's wife, Farrokh, was there. I had known him before leaving Iran and would help him with his school of management papers, as my English was better than his. He called and said he would be arrested and would have to go fight in the Iran-Iraq war if he stayed in Iran. I thought, *Why not? I will have a husband. He will be rescued from going to war. And if God is willing, I'll have a child.* I didn't want to replace Babak but to keep me busy before going crazy over missing him. A lot of women these days get frozen eggs and sperm just to have a child on their own so no one can claim the child. That was kind of unheard of at that time.

I flew to Iran for a short visit and made a big mistake, a very big mistake. I married him. His name was Farrokh.

My father thought he was a good man and educated and handsome. He dressed well. I was not in love with him, but I liked him well enough. He would follow me to Geneva. He and his parents came to ask for my hand. I was crying before they came, and my father asked me why.

I said, "I miss Babak. I feel I am cheating him."

They shook their head, as they did not know why I was different. I did not and do not know why I do things. The best book I read about that was called *Why Do I Do That?* by Joseph Burgo. I read it just recently but too late—as is always the case in life, too late.

I went to Iran with that purpose. I heard more dirty words from my sister's husband. I hated him and felt so bad around him. He even brought his newborn daughter, Yasi, and put this baby in the back seat of the car and suggested that he would take me to the passport office. On the road, he kept telling me, "Please let me love you," as if he needed permission from me, even in his dreams, to be disloyal to his wife, thinking of another woman. Shamefully, his wife was my sister.

I stopped giving my sister hints about what was going on, as she was totally convinced that it was not her husband but me who was pursuing this connection. How one can fool her mind to believe whatever she prefers to believe? I am sure there is a terminology in psychology for that.

I got married in a beige dress, at Farrokh's parents' house. It was a short ceremony, and in the middle of the party, sirens were heard, announcing the planes of the enemy were in Tehran's sky. We had to finish quickly. We went upstairs, and I spent the night in Farrokh's flat, which was on the second floor of the same house. We decorated it together.

But as I opened my eyes the next morning, Farrokh looked at me and said, "You have been robbed" (*Saret kola raft*). I was surprised and shocked. I also saw some literature about homosexuality next to his bed. But my mind played the same trick with me as my sister's mind does to her. I denied the signs and the truth.

In two days, I flew back to Switzerland and made an appointment with Mlle Bertchi. She was very angry with me when I said I had gotten married and needed a visa for my new husband. She said, "This guy is not at your level. It's not a true match, and you should not have gotten married." She also said " look at me, I was not married because I had not found my match."

I told myself, if it wasn't a match, there was still merit in the union. First, I'd rescued someone from going to war and getting killed. Second, I might have a child with him, and maybe that would fill some of the void in my heart, yearning for my son. Both logics were wrong, but I was young and restless and only twenty-nine.

I had to change lawyers, as Mlle Bertchi refused to take my case. I got a gentleman as my lawyer, and he got Farrokh a visa. Farrokh came to Geneva with his sister and his sister's husband. We all stayed in my little studio. I was working at the digital company and took some days off. We took my in-laws sightseeing, and I liked his sister a lot.

After a couple of days they left. Farrokh would stay home, and I would go to work. He refused to apply for any jobs except management positions. Who would hire him for management positions with his qualifications? He knew not a word of French, and his English was not good either. Day by day, I saw that I had made such a mistake.

My job sent me to the United States for a mission. I took Farrokh with me. We visited my brother and his wife, who is a relative of Farrokh. He obviously loved the United States, and his only purpose was to get there.

So-called, short married life

We returned to Geneva, and Farrokh was getting further and further away from me. He was a closeted gay man, and I did not know that yet. I thought having problems in life and staying home had made him depressed. One day he said he wanted to go to the United States and did not like living in Geneva. I said I'd had it. It wasn't easy to establish a visa and a job at that time, and I had both. I called my father and a relative, Mahmoud Khan, who was a lawyer and asked them to arrange for my divorce without my being physically present there, as I had no intention of returning to Iran. They did.

Since I had gotten Farrokh the visa for Switzerland, he could get a visa for the United States through Switzerland. He wanted to shake hands with me, and I was so angry that I turned away and let him out of my house. I was happy that I had not gotten pregnant. I did not know that I would never get pregnant again, as if God was punishing me for the dear son I'd had and had not stayed with, however miserable my life would have been. My logic was that my son was happy with Bahman and his family and would not be happy with me and my mother—two angry women. Of course, I also knew Bahman's would get another lawyer and wouldn't let me have him.

After Farrokh left, I had a mini nervous breakdown. I missed my son and was contemplating how I could get to Canada and get a job and live there all by myself in an unknown country. I called my brother in Washington, DC, and he said, "Go for walks in the mornings. And if you are so sad and alone in Geneva, come to the United States."

One day as I was sitting in front of my computer at the digital company in Geneva, I started crying and crying. I resigned that day, sold my car and the few belongings I had in that studio, and went to Paris via TGV train to visit a friend, Nasi. I saw Mansoor, the guy who had taken me to the airport and who I liked. In

Paris, while crying and being depressed, I had a short visit with him. I don't know how, in that age of no cell phones and no internet, we found each other. But I remember our visit at Nasi's house. He taught me to think of the universe and how small we and our problems are compared to where we are in the universe. It calmed me down but did not affect the part of missing my son.

CHAPTER 33

A SURPRISE HOUSE GUEST

I returned to Geneva to sell the last items I had and buy a ticket to fly to the United States. I could not go back to Iran, as I did not want to see my sister's no-good husband again. Also when I would call Iran to talk to my mother, he would jump up and answer the phone and bother me with his usual words of how much he loved me. He was like a snake. He did all of that making sure my sister would not see it or hear of it.

I returned from Paris to Geneva a day earlier than expected. I had given my house key to a friend to look after my cat while I was visiting Paris. When I opened the door, I saw a woman sleeping in my bed. I was angry, but that was how they were taking care of my house. I said, "Who are you?"

She said, "My name is Guity, and I've just come to Switzerland. I'm waiting to get a visa to go to the United States." She told me about her husband, Moe, an activist in the confederation society, which I knew about from my time at Purdue. She also said they were divorced and she though he was now dating an American woman in America.

I said, "Seems like all confederation people are in trouble now, instead of getting the benefit of this revolution—all except the extreme fanatics and mullahs who are taking advantage of the revolution. The rest are not happy."

Before going to bed, she said, "A friend called Mamak is a friend of my husband." I knew a Mamak, which was a very odd name—almost nonexistent—who was a friend of my sister.

I said, "Which Mamak? The one married to Mahin?"

She said, "Oh yes, the architect, and Moe is an architect too."

I said, "Wow. Then we know each other somehow," and started trusting her.

I saw her for the last days that I stayed in Geneva, and we talked and laughed. In the end, she gave me her husband's number, and I told her I would find out about Moe.

I was trying to give my cat away before I left Switzerland and put an ad in the elevator of my building. People would call and ask about my Persian cat. I would tell them, "I am Persian. My cat is not born from me. She is not Persian. She's just an ordinary short-haired cat."

Cats and I are always together. But in my story now, I was leaving Switzerland and all the people I know there. I called Shahnaz, Shahla, and Linie and said goodbye. I said goodbye to Nasi and Pierre, a French computer boy I knew already in Paris.

I was getting closer to my son. He lived in Canada, and I was going to the United States. I felt a little happier in my heart. I was asking God, Would there ever be a day that we live in the same country, me and my dear son?

The answer was yes, but it would be years and years and years between now and that point. And sadly, after we got closer to each other, the visitations stayed almost the same as before—becoming even shorter in duration.

CHAPTER 34

BABAK'S VISITATIONS, 1984 ON AFTER

As soon as I arrived in the United States and landed in Washington, DC, I looked at the map and saw the part of Canada Bahman and Babak were in—Vancouver. That was above California, and I was in Virginia, on the East Coast, close to Montreal and Toronto. Not that I could travel to either places and was allowed to leave the United States and return. Still, the fact that I was closer to my son—having gone from continents apart to countries apart—was a relief.

I called Bahman and asked him whether I could meet them in Washington state in a border city. He said they could drive there. I flew there and stayed in a hotel room. He drove from Canada and brought Babak, who was six or seven years old. It was his birthday, so it must have been the month of April. I hugged him and kissed him. He knew me and did not run away, and the three of us went to a Chinese restaurant. For a day, things seemed normal.

They returned the next day, and life was dull again. Bahman said he couldn't send Babak every year. He claimed he didn't have the money to get a ticket to send him to DC. I said I will pay for the ticket and reminded him that it was my right to see my son once a year. I didn't want to remind him that, according to the divorce papers, he was to pay for a yearly visit. I always tried to be nice to him so I could see my son. To this day, he still claims he doesn't have money and never paid for Babak's yearly visits to America.

I would come back. But I started the year like a zombie and made wrong decisions in terms of relationship, until I got my green card.

Before getting the green card, I would live the year with the hope of Babak's one-week or five-day visits. I would change my whole lifestyle for those days that my little boy would fly all alone from Canada to DC. A flight attendant would give him to me. Then I would beg all the people I knew with little children to come to my house so that he would have a nice visit, so he would not say no to coming over the next year. He was the king of the house. With him around, I could see other children and not cry. But from the day he was supposed to leave to one week after, I would start crying and gradually change back to a life with no happiness, except a boyfriend to make me forget the pain.

Every time I would think of him and wondering, *By whom and how is he fed? What does he do when he gets sick? How is he treated?* I was glad that his grandparents were close by. If Bahman, being a man, would be busy dating or doing this and that, my son would not be neglected. Only one thing was good, and that was the fact that his parents did not quarrel like mine had.

I would call every week, but half the time Babak was not available. He was fishing with his father, gone to an island. I would hang up and cry. Once I asked him, "Can you call me?" He said no. He was too little, and text messaging or internet or cell phones did not yet exist.

After I got my green card, immediately I made arrangements to go to Canada. From the United States, I talked to a lawyer about settling my visitation rights so I would not be at the mercy of Bahman and his family to send Babak. I needed to have some law on my side, especially as we were not in Iran anymore, and I had more rights as a woman than that stupid religious regime in Iran allowed. The law there said sons went to their fathers at the age of two, and girls were to stays with their mother only till they were seven years of age, at which point they were returned to their fathers. Usually, fathers gave the children to the mothers. But here that was not the case. I had a job, citizenship. and all and could afford to have my son back with me or at least get more visitations.

When I heard that Babak's father had married Natasha, who had a boy and that they were having a son called Dara, I wanted to go and see where he lived and how my son was treated by his stepmother.

I found out that I had a relative called Yazdan in Vancouver. I called him and asked him to let me stay there for a week. He was a bachelor and very young but with a golden heart. He let me in. His parents used to live across the alley in Darrous with us, and his grandma was my father's aunt. She was the sister of Aghajoon Parsay; had blue, blue eyes; and we called her Ammeh Khanium. Actually his name, Yazdan Bakhsh, meaning "God granted him to us," was given to him by my father.

I asked Bahman to see their new house where Babak lived. I remember seeing Natasha, a nice beautiful girl, and Bahman standing at the door with her holding a child. I passed through after a formal hello and found out that Babak was living in the attic, and the rest of the family was downstairs. There was a sunny room on the first floor. I asked them to move Babak to that room and treat him like a king. That was the only thing I could do for him. And I left that house quickly.

Then I called my lawyer, a Canadian woman who I'd found through an American lawyer. She said she wanted to see me and my son together. I took my son with me. He was eight maybe. He said, "I don't want to see a lawyer. I will not talk against my father."

"You don't have to say anything you don't want to," I told him. "Nothing will be said against your father. This is only to secure our yearly meetings."

We met the kind and nice lawyer. She totally understood me. She felt my suffering and asked a couple of simple questions. I guess she wanted to make sure that my son liked to visit me and that I was not a drunk or abusive mother.

Afterward, she said, "I'm sure that all is on your side. But since they live in Canada, your lawyer must be a Canadian, not an American. But I assure you, you have your visitation rights, and it is done."

I have a picture of my son holding himself next to his father and one with me in Yazdan's house. If it wasn't for the pictures, I don't know how I would remember the chronology of events. I flew back hoping I had not damaged my relationship with my son. In his little mind, I hoped he was not afraid of hurting his father. Deep in my heart, I wanted him to love and obey his father, so he would be raised right. I tried to always say good things about his father and encourage him to solve his problems through his father and his family. After all, he was living there 90 percent of the time.

What happened next shattered my heart again. The news came that, shortly after we met the lawyer, she died of pneumonia. My luck. I was back to square one. I was again under Bahman's family's mercy to send Babak, and they weren't paying for the trip expenses either.

Bahman's second divorce

A year after that, Babak called me for the first time one day. *How strange*, I thought. I asked him, "What's wrong ?"

"It's okay," he said. "I'm in the street calling you from a pay phone. Bahman and Natasha are getting a divorce."

I was shocked and sad and wanted to cry. I had to decide quickly. Should I blame his father or what? Would it be okay to separate him from his school and friends and bring him to me? Plus, my heart was broken that he was seeing another divorce and I didn't know if this one was amicable like ours had been. I was also sure that Bahman's family would get a lawyer and fight me if I tried to get custody. And I would have to get another Canadian lawyer until Babak was eighteen.

I decided to back Bahman up because Babak had to listen to him as an authority figure. I said, "I am sorry, but whatever you feel, discuss it with your father. He wants the best for you," and hung up. I cried and cried. The one time he needed me most, I had nothing to say and not do anything.

Natasha and Bahman divorced, and Bahman got custody of his second son, Dara. I was jealous that he had two sons, and I had none.

Later, he married again and had another son. Now he has three sons, and I have a part-time son with hourly visitations up to this day. But I am glad for however long and however often I see him. I am getting ahead of myself.

I had to always have a good job, and it was back to survival mode. In my life, my priority was always to have a good job and, in order to keep my sanity, have a friend around me to keep me forgetting about my heart, which felt so miserable without my son. If only I had known how difficult these feelings were, I would have never chosen women's independence. I would have been happy just being around my son and obeying the rules of the society enforced upon women!

I was afraid to go live in Canada, though now that I had US citizenship, I could do that. However, I'd already started a new life from zero in Switzerland and then done so again in the United States. I didn't have the courage or the energy to start yet again from zero. I was trying to pass time till Babak was eighteen and could decide for himself to come to the United States.

How little I knew. The longer he stayed there, the more damage was done to our relationship and engraved in his brain. I started hating Canada. When anybody would say the word *Canada*, I would become immediately angry. When my son would call himself Canadian, I would get furious. I was hoping for a day that he would become American and live in the same country with me.

CHAPTER 35

SO-CALLED VISITATION WITH MY SON

My life went on, and I would see my son once a year for five to seven days. Add it up, and after forty years, it's still less than 365 days. Sometimes my mother was around. Shaahin, my brother's son, was always around. Children, if they were relatives and friends his age, were welcome to my house whether they had good manners or not. I thought four days in a year would not hurt his behavior, and maybe he would learn to be street smart.

A boy called Moe and Farnoosh, a relative's daughter, and Shirin, daughter of Kami, an old and dear friend, were there at different years. Pictures show this. I made sure that, every year he came over, we went to the Sears store and took a picture. I would enlarge the photo and live with looking at that picture for the whole year, until his next visitation. There are pictures of him with Tina, the daughter of Tye who I met in Richmond, half American and half Iranian; with Shahnaz, my friend from Geneva; with my brother and Roya, parents of Shaahin; and, of course, with my mother on different years. Like any child, he grew to love his grandma more than his mother. I was that way too, so like mother, like son.

At every visit, I would sit in my car waiting for his plane to take off and crying for an hour. I would have to switch back and forth emotionally. I was mostly sad and would just put a brave face on to enable me to go to work and make money and survive and pay for my son's visits. A cousin, Kourosh, who lived in Canada with his kind wife, Marie, upon my request, sent me some Canadian stamps. I sent them in a letter to my son and asked, "Can you send letters sometimes? And here are the stamps to use." He never did. I am not sure if he ever got that letter. Any child in the street would remind me of him, and going to a kid's school was off of my schedule totally. I did not know what the kids did at school, whose birthday it was, or what parents did going to games and all. I could not bear it. I made the wrong decision when I chose to stay away from that hurt by soothing myself in a relationship.

At another point, when I was between jobs, I asked Mrs. Kolbadi, a friend of my mother and my schoolteacher of English, to fly to Oregon to visit her relatives and then rent a car and drive to Vancouver. I had to see where Babak was living with a new stepmother called Terry.

Going to Vancouver

We flew to Oregon, stayed with a relative of Mrs. Kolbadi, went to a Baha'i wedding, and then rented a car to drive to Vancouver. I saw a Baha'i marriage in Oregon for the first time, and it was nice. I saw Oregon for the first time in my life. I asked some authorities there about my visitation rights and the payments. They said it was unfortunate, but they couldn't do anything about it. General Sanii was considered a very popular and powerful figure in the Baha'i faith, although he broke the law for Baha'is that says a Baha'i cannot be a politician. Staying away from politics is a must, but working for the UN or the environment was encouraged. Bahman's father got an exemption called "Tarde Edaree" from Baha'i community authorities. So again, I submitted to my destiny and was happy and nervous going there.

Vancouver reminded me of Switzerland. Mrs. Kolbadi and I found my former in-laws' house in a beautiful area overlooking the ocean. General Sanii and Touri Joon, my son's grandparents, greeted us, and I faced my son as a grown-up little man, becoming a teenager.

Bahaman had just gotten married to this Canadian/American girl, and she was pregnant. Touri Joon did not approve of that marriage, but Bahman was about to have his third son, from his third marriage. The wife was in the kitchen, and Bahman was in the living room. We all sat down and talked a while. Then I asked

Bahman, "Would you join us for lunch?" I added quietly, "It is good for Babak to see that his parents are on good terms and have lunch together for an hour."

He went to the kitchen to ask his new wife, Terry. She said no.

I almost begged Bahman, saying, "Please explain to your wife that this is a once-in-a-lifetime event and for one hour only."

Bahman went back to the kitchen to consult her.

General Sanii looked at me and said, "Bahman's wife is you, always." That touched me. I saw that Babak had witnessed that.

Bahman came back and said no again.

I took Babak, and we went to a restaurant with Mrs. Kolbadi. I was very angry with Bahman—for not paying for any expenses; for not helping out with visitations; and also for, having been a mama's boy, now having become a wife's boy. It was not easy for me to get off work and go to Canada. Staying in a hotel in a city I did not know anything about was not easy either. We spent some time in the street adjacent to their house, taking pictures in that street, and we left on a ferry that afternoon. Leaving Babak was getting harder and harder every time. We left that evening, and my heart was left in Vancouver as we got farther and farther from the shore. I was back to living like a zombie and making wrong decisions, except when it came to job opportunities. I never was out of a job for more than two weeks. I will explain that later, but this chapter focuses on visits with my son.

CHAPTER 36

LIFE GOES ON

I returned to DC and went back to work. Moe, my architect and leftist friend, helped me, lending me $3,000 dollars for a down payment on my apartment in Alexandria. I bought that condo in a high-rise on the twelfth floor. I met a woman called Mary there, and up to now, we are of best friends. I also paid Moe back in a couple of months by getting a loan from a bank. I did not want to be obliged to see him because of the money that he'd lent me. We became friends, though his daughter disagreed with our making it more serious, and I did not want to push it. Moe died of leukemia without a wife. Somehow he was too stingy to forgive his wife, Guity(that I met in Geneva), for throwing away a bottle of milk. He was super smart in politics but backward in some areas of life. I went my way and kept visiting my son once a year.

I have a picture of my son and my mother in DC, and he is a tall teenager. He was involved with computers and studying. My mother had cancer and was wearing those turbans you wear when you've lost your hair due to chemotherapy. Life was not easy. At one point, I got a roommate in that small one-bedroom place. After that, I had several roommates, even a twenty-year-old African boy. He would use this medicine for his hair that, to my eyes, changed nothing about its appearance and only smelled. Another African girl had a boyfriend, and I did not like it. A white girl was sloppy. But I needed money, especially when I was between jobs, to save so I could bring my son over for our annual visits.

At last I rented my house to a Russian girl and went to Germantown in Maryland and became a roommate of Shohreh, a friend. There I met Daria, a Jewish boy, who was weird but funny, and I really liked him at that time. I have a picture of Babak and him too. I'll get to that later. Here, I am concentrating on my son's visitations, and events overlap when you focus on each event in your life from different angles.

I also have pictures of my son at the birthday party of Farnoosh, a cousin's daughter. He was getting older. I am wearing an ugly orange dress that my mother sewed from an Indian material. I was still under my mother's control, and she had cancer. I will explain my mother's life and that part of my life's story when I write a chapter about my mother.

Every year, I sent Babak tickets, and he came over for less than a week. He got to be old enough to have talks with me, but he refused to hear any explanations about what had happened to cause his father and I to get divorced. I was totally blamed for everything in his mind. After all, he lived with people who did not say good things about me. When he was younger, he once told me, "When I was born, my father was the first to see me and hold me." Well, I had a C-section. He even said something to the effect of, "Boys are born from men." I let it pass.

At another visit, he said, "I hate teachers and poor people. How come none of your relatives are rich?"

Well, my mother, my aunt, and I were teachers, and we were not as wealthy as his father. But his rich father never paid for his tickets or school. I could not explain those things to him. I just let it go so that he would love his father and listen to him and be raised properly. I made a mistake, not defending myself, as the idea that I was the guilty one and the lower one became permanent in his mind.

He also in another visit said, "You were having a man in the house!" When I confronted him and his father at his graduation time in Cornell, he said, " I made it up." As usual, Bahman said, "I don't recall."

Men don't recall whatever they don't want to face—like my sister and her husband. I let all those comments pass by. Only twice did I see a good reaction out of my son. Once, I took him to the airport, and we took pictures. In one, I was posing like a sexy gesture. Then something happened to the plane and it was delayed. When he came back, he had put that sexy picture in an envelope to give to his father. His little mind was trying. It broke my heart like crazy. I should not complain of my heart being broken, as his was broken way more than mine. Children are the only victims of a divorce, and there are so many of them all over the world. And I am a product of divorce times three.

CHAPTER 37

BABAK MOVED TO AMERICA AND HIS GRADUATION

The good thing was for continuing his education Babak chose to go to Cornell. That brought him to the same country but different states. As I was in heaven being closer to him, he was being kinder to me. The other incident when I saw a positive reaction from Babak toward me centered on a man I had seriously dated and then married for a year, after twelve years of not being married. Babak showed a sign of jealousness. He walked between me and this guy. Maybe Babak, being a man himself, knew something. The guy's name was Mehrdad (unfortunately, the same name as my sister's husband, so for a while I called him another name).

We got married for comfort and convenience, but I liked his poetry abilities and that he was a professor. He knew how to impress me with knowledge. He was four years younger than me and had a lot of psychological problems. I will explain that divorce later, but during the short time that I was married to him (for a year), I saw Babak the most. This was partially because Babak's friend's mother and her second husband lived in Maryland. I loved that period because I had a house, and we looked like normal people. I was married, and he could visit me with family around me. I did not have to change my whole lonely life for a period of a week because he was visiting me. I could continue with the hope of seeing him next.

Babak graduated, and I went to Cornell to celebrate his graduation. Bahman came from Canada, and we both felt so proud witnessing our son's graduation from a great school. All his professors had great things to say about him. I did not know that his father wasn't paying a penny for his studies and that Babak himself was working to pay for the student loan he had. I was not rich myself. And I never thought that, with all the wealth Bahman and his family had, Babak would have to be in debt for so long. For that, I don't forgive them, though I've expressed my thankfulness for the years they brought him up and all. Being stingy was characteristic of Bahman and his father.

Babak helped me pack my stuff after I got divorced from Mehrdad, a very stupid act and another major wrong thing I did. Babak helped me to put my stuff in a moving storage. I'll go into detail about that very short one year marriage later, but I was soooo, soooo sad that he had to witness that stupid divorce. If I had only known that my son would have to endure his father's divorces and mine too, I would have shut up and lived in a house on the same street as my in-laws lived in Canada. But life teaches you experiences too late for a rewind.

Babak decided to continue his studies in California at the University of Davis. That was why I left DC for California. He actually got his PhD there, and I am proud to have such a clever son. I asked Dick Holmberg, a friend and former coworker who looks just like my paternal grandpa with blue eyes, to help me drive a huge U-Haul style vehicle towing my car to California. At last I was going to live in the same state as my son. We'd gotten ever closer—from the same continent to the same country and now the same state.

Babak was close to thirty years old when that happened. He'd just met his girlfriend Claudia, at UC Davis, whose sister was a student there. Babak and Claudia dated for a while, and then they got married. We'll get to that later too. I even got to go to his graduation and felt so proud it was unimaginable. There were Claudia and I in that ceremony. I was so excited that I only got Babak a present and forgot to get something for Claudia. I apologized to Claudia for not getting her a present, and she said, "Don't worry. I am getting a PhD man." She was too clever for me.

My visits were still short and seven to eight months apart, but at least I could feel better being closer to him.

One big change that happened after I moved to California and got much closer to my son was that I didn't have a close relationship with any man. This has been true now for seventeen years, and I feel so good and fulfilled that I don't need a wrong relationship. I don't feel as empty as I did when I was farther away from my son. I can see an exact relationship between the distance between me and my son and the wrong relationship decisions I was making—feeling so desperate, empty, and sad. The power of being able to see your son is a way better treatment for the heart than anything.

CHAPTER 38

DURING SEPARATIONS FROM MY CHILD

Once Babak came over, and on the advice of my therapist, I asked him, "Who do you think is your mother?"

He simply said, "You."

I succeeded in making him understand that, no matter what, he was my son, I loved him, and I would do anything for him. The truth was I never left him in my heart. I felt relieved that, even though I had missed his birthdays—even on the phone because his father and my in-laws would say, "He is not available," or, "He's gone fishing in an island"—and even though we have lived so far from each other, my persistence had paid off. I had accepted any humiliation, cold shoulders, and all and had kept calling and bringing him to see me.

I tried to help him see that he did have a family who loved him on his mother's side. He loved my brother Farzad a lot and his wife, Roya. He loved my mother a lot. He doesn't remember my father. he left Iran when he was two and a half years old, and my father never traveled to America. His uncles and aunt do not go visit him. They are not talking to me, let alone my son. The few times that I could see him with them were during the Persian New Year's parties at my cousin Nahid's house in Bel Air.

They stopped inviting me due to the clash with my sister and her husband. I could not tell them how important their presence was for me during any small window that I found to see my son. I don't forgive any of them for doing that to me, especially my sister and her husband. I was living for the days that I had the smallest opportunity to see Babak, and they took that away from me. They all ganged up against me because I was a whistleblower. I was so anxious to see my son once a year for Norooz that sometimes I would drive a week earlier from Monterey to Bel Air anticipating his visit. I was so anxious to see him that I would mix up the weeks.

During the New Year parties, I was told by relatives to leave my son alone—to pretend as if our reunion was not that important and to give him space. He should mingle with his friends his age. No one understood me, as none of them missed so many birthdays, Christmases, and Thanksgivings with their children. I was so thirsty—driven to the water—and was not allowed to drink.

I don't know if anyone out there understands me. Divorce happens, but nothing prepares you for the separation from your child. Sometimes I would watch Babak from the corner of the room and send him kisses in the air without him knowing. I was trying to act cool and listen to those who had "successful marriages and successful relationships with their kids."

It took me years and years to notice how isolated I was from any kids. The realization struck me when my son was twenty-something years old, maybe around 1999. I was living with Mehrdad, my last husband, and I was driving in Falls Church, Virginia, when a ball hit my car and dropped in front of my car. I looked up, and there was this Catholic school next to my house and kids playing in the ground. The ball they were playing with fell in front of my car, and I felt happy and, for the first time, had no fear when I looked at the school kids—children of all different ages.

I walked into that school and asked whether I could volunteer. I watched every day a different boy in a different age bracket and thought of him as Babak at that age and in school. That was a therapy for me—better late than never.

CHAPTER 39

DEATH OF GRANDMA ZINAT JOON, 1992

I went to Iran in 1992 to visit my grandma for the last time. I had eleven months between seeing Babak every year, and I could spare some months to first see my fathers grave and also see my grandma for the last time.

Before my return from that trip—a last visit to Iran for a short four months—a nice event happened that brought all my grandma's children together. She was sick and in her bed, and I invited all my uncles and their wives and my mother to her little studio. We all gathered around her bed, and we sang a song called "Shod Khazan." This was sung by a famous singer called Badizadeh, who was my grandma's cousin. Grandma could play violin and sing and recite simple poetry. My Uncle Houshang took after her, liking the arts. We all sang around her bed and, in the end, Maman said to me, "Roya that was great, but now I am tired. Please ask them to leave."

I motioned to all. They all left, and she thanked me and went to sleep.

She also would eat lots of grease and fat. She ended up being ninety-two or ninety-three before she died. So go figure—all these theories about sugar and fat consumption. She also smoked tobacco on the hookah. But at one point when she was sick, she said, " I think it's because I was playing violin and singing in my youth."

I said, "Maman, being ninety-something is hardly called a punishment for what you did at youth."

The superstitions that feed us in childhood are forever with us.

Exactly three months after I returned to the United States, Maman Zinat Joon died. The day before I left Tehran, in 1992, I went to her studio. She was lying on the floor beside the heater. She just said, "I am told not to talk to you."

My mother and sister made sure Maman would not change my mind. They figured I had become an American now, and I should return to the United States and continue to live and work there. I had reached the same conclusion. If only my son was in America, then returning would be easier. But returning to an empty nest in youth is painful.

But every day of living with my grandma had been precious too. I knew I would only see my son once a year, so I had time. I'd stayed four months, and now I had to leave. I lay next to her on the floor, and for a long, long time we stayed that way without saying a word.

Sometime later, my uncle's wife, Soraya Joon, came up the stairs to her studio, looked at us, and quietly left. She understood how much we both loved each other—my grandma and I. That was the last time I saw her. We did not have FaceTime then. On her deathbed, I managed a phone call, and she said "I am okay." But I guess that was what she was told to say too.

I wish that she and my grandpa are having a cup of tea under a tree in heaven together. Kisses for them always.

I am glad I made that trip since I visited my father's grave and paid my respect to him.

CHAPTER 40

MOTHER'S BREAST AND, LATER, BLADDER CANCER, 1993–2001

Once when my mother came to Alexandria, Virginia, to visit, she acted a bit different. We were going to a party at a high-rise at my mother's cousin's. As we were waiting in the lobby of my cousin Fereshteh's house in Virginia, she said, "I need to tell you something."

"What?" I asked. "Right now, before the party begins?"

"I have this thing in my breast."

"What thing?"

"I will show you when we go in."

I was surprised. She was breaking big news in the middle of a party? I guess she'd been hiding it for so long that she just burst then and there, though my sister and Uncle Farhang and his wife, Soraya Joon knew about it.

When we got inside, I took her to a room and said, "What is it? Show me."

She pulled her bra down, and I saw a big red spot on her breast. The stage when you can see the tumor is a long time passed the stage when a spot might be found during a mammogram.

"What were you doing in Iran?" I asked. "Why didn't you see a doctor?"

"Well, I was hiding it," she told me. "I did not want to bother anyone. It's maybe nothing."

I talked to my uncle's wife, Soraya Joon, later. She said it was close to the death of my grandma, my mother's mother, when the lump had first been discovered.

She had been complaining that she had some pain in her right hand. They thought she'd broken her hand sometime ago falling in her kitchen. Then Soraya Joon, who worked as an aid in my uncle's office and would examine the women, learned from Uncle Farhang that my mother was experiencing pain. She had her lie down and examined her. After the examination, she ran downstairs to their house. My uncle was sad, knowing that he would soon lose his mother, but Soraya Joon said, "We have a bigger problem right now. I think Shokouh" (my mother) "has breast cancer." As it was customary, and customs always win, my mother waited to look into her own issues, to first take care of her mother. My grandma died, they buried her, and then that was when my mother decided to come to the United States to have her treatment and operation here. Hospitals and sanitary conditions in Iran weren't good at that time.

I agreed. But like always, I had been the last to know. My sister was greatly skilled at hiding everything from me, even something like this that would require a change of schedule for all of us. I was furious.

I called to get her an appointment with my doctor who had done my mammogram, and the receptionist said he was booked. I took her with me to the office and said, "I want the doctor to see this and decide when to give us an appointment."

As soon as the doctor saw her breast, he immediately did the mammogram. The results were obvious. She had advanced cancer of the right breast. He said it may have spread to her underarms and looked at us as if we were coming from another planet. Who would wait this long to see a doctor? I kept quiet, but in my mind, I was saying, *You don't know our mother.* She was strong and never let anything break her. Part of it was because she was a hardheaded woman. Maybe Cat Stevens should have married her if he was looking for a hardheaded woman! And part of it was something called *aberoo* (honor)—like, "What would people say?" Even the dumbest people are considered important when one says, "What would people say?" All over the world, so many people keep quiet, just being afraid that their honor will be spilled if they speak up. That attitude and the fact that some strong traditions are behind stupid practices, like fundamental ideas, always win in society as the majority.

The news was discussed with my brother and his wife. They played a great role in the process of her treatment by letting her stay with them. I was living in a one-bedroom apartment, and they had a house. Also, they had their own reasons for doing so. We all went to the Reston Hospital, and she was operated on. It was the hardest day of my life. We waited for hours and hours. I was praying in front of the hospital in a parking lot. After half an hour of praying and talking to God and begging him, I saw a figure that moved in a car. This person had been watching me the entire time, and I had thought I was alone—crying and talking to God. I felt ashamed and returned to the hospital.

The surgery took five hours. The surgical team said the cancer had spread to all her lymph nodes under her arm, and the doctors removed her right breast. My mother had large breasts, and we were thinking, *How will it look?* We were facing problems and events that we had no knowledge of. We hadn't seen anyone with this problem before and did not know much about cancer.

She was brought back to her room. The doctor called us. In the lobby of the hospital, where Farzad and Roya and I had been waiting, we all gathered around him. He explained that the cancer had spread. He would not answer how long she had, would not answer how the ending would be, whether it would be painful, or what we could do about it. He just said, "Take care of her," and advised that she would need heavy-duty chemotherapy.

I know how my brother felt because I was in the same boat. We'd never had her sick. It was always my mother who took care of us. She was a strong person to lean on. We were not leaned on. She was the one we took care of us. She was our rock. That was why both of us left as soon as she was brought into the room and was out of anesthesia. We left her with Roya, my brother's wife. We were going to face her tomorrow when she woke up.

I went back to Alexandria but, by the middle of the night, could take it no longer and drove back to the hospital and released Roya to go home and sleep. I stood by my mother. I saw the nurse talking to her and telling her that she had cancer. I hated it that, in the United States, the doctors explain every detail. As she was going into the operation room, the doctor explained that they would put a tube in her mouth and do this and that. I only translated this to my mother as, "First, the doctors will put you to sleep. Then, they'll operate on you, and you'll come out."

We also found out that Mother has a reaction to morphine. I was worried because I'd always heard that, when the pain starts for cancer patients, the only thing that works is morphine. When the doctors stopped the morphine after she came out of the operating room, she got better.

I explained to her what had happened to her—that the surgeons had removed one breast and some lymph nodes from under her arm.

She said, "It would be better if they removed both of my breasts." She was right, as one side was a big breast and the other side was none. We had not seen any pictures of those who underwent breast cancer operations and did not know where to find a special bra or even if a bra like that existed. This was thirty years ago, and we were all young and inexperienced too.

My brother and Roya took Mother to their house. And again, since I could not bear changing her bandages, we asked Roya for help. If you are one step farther away from a relative, it is easier, and she did a great job. She would take the bandages that drained blood, and we would all laugh, calling them Dracula's tea bags. We tried to make Mother feel as if nothing major had happened.

Then the day came for her chemotherapy. Again I would go right after they brought her back home and stay with her, but I couldn't stand seeing the nurses put needles in her. I would look away when they put needles in my son on routine visits to doctors during his childhood too. I learned that people who take care of cancer patients need to take strong pills and/or alcohol because the patient is given drugs, and the people around the patient are left alone. I started smoking and drinking. As soon as her chemo was finished, I suggested that my brother make his garage into a room and add a shower and get permission to do it. His wife disagreed. She was willing to help but never wanted to change her house to make it comfortable for a sick person to live there. I don't blame her. They bought a bigger house later, but again, the basement had everything except a bathroom and shower.

So I decided to take Mother to live with me. I rented out my one-bedroom in Alexandria and rented a three-bedroom in Falls Church. I also rented one room to a student so I could afford it. Mother was in one room listening on a radio I got for her, an all-Persian station called Radio Iran. She would listen to it in her room and sometimes would ask me to listen to it with her, but I refused. Later I would listen to Radio Iran a lot, but that was way later.

My mother only watched *Days of Our Lives* on TV, with her broken English. Since the time I was at Purdue and Mother would visit me she would watch that show. I never watched it, but somehow that story never ended. She would go back to Iran and return after months or years and still could follow the *Days of Our Lives*. My brother Farhad once said, "Do you see this baby is born now? Next year when mother returns, this baby will be the mother of the guy delivering her."

We laughed. But in our hearts we were crying, since Mother was in remission, and we did not know how long she would be alive. After a year and as usual, Mother got bored and wanted to leave. Although she would visit my two brothers in San Diego and Reston often, she flew back to Iran. I returned to my apartment in Alexandria.

Mother's story

Since this chapter is all about my mother, I will tell her story. She was cured from breast cancer. But the chemotherapy went to her bladder and gave her cancer of the bladder. This happened close to five years of remission or as soon as I was celebrating in my heart that mother had been cured. She was bleeding and hiding it.

When my uncle, who was a heart physician in Tehran, and my uncle's wife's brother, Mehran, diagnosed it, they decided to send her back to the United States. This time, my brother lived in Ashburn, Virginia, and I was in Alexandria, Virginia. I rented an apartment for her on a floor above mine. She could have her visitors and all. I would do her laundry and whatever else needed done in my apartment, and she would cook upstairs, and friends and family would visit her.

She was having some problems. Uncle Houshang came over. I got him some painting materials and asked him to paint some scenery for me. I still have that painting hanging in my room. Mahin Banoo, the aunt and friend of my mother, would stay with her.

Finally, her doctors decided to operate on her. They would take the bladder out and insert a bag in place of it. My mother would make a joke and say, "I put a sign down there that says, 'The store is completely closed,'" as she would have most of her glands removed.

The day of her operation, which was the day my mother's female doctor who had recommended the operation got married, she had an abnormal heart rate. Dr. Mahnaz was too busy with her marriage ceremony and ordered the operation. Some Chinese doctor recommended not going ahead with it, but no one listened.

After the surgical team took her to the operation room, I got separated from Farzad and Roya. I was walking in the corridors of the hospital, and then I decided to have a cup of tea, so I went to the cafeteria. It was only half past the time I left them. There were cell phones then. But much to my surprise, I saw that the two male doctors who were supposed to be doing the operation were sitting down in the cafeteria and eating. I approached them and asked, "What happened?"

They were surprised and said, "You don't know?"

I replied, "No. What happened?"

"Well, she had some heart complications, and we had to stop the operation. We opened her but had to close her up without touching her bladder."

I ran upstairs. My brother and his wife knew what had happened but never called me. I did not know what to do. Why did they all behave like this toward me? My sister wouldn't give me the news of my mother's illness in the first place. Now, my brother and his wife did this. They only wanted to have my name on the schedule of who took care of Mother and at what time. I was just a moving body.

I ran to her room. She was in ICU and in coma. I called my uncle in Iran on my cell phone. I was screaming, "Uncle Farhang, they have mother almost upside down. She is in coma. All the doctors in the ICU are working on her."

My uncle said, "If she is in the ICU, they know what they are doing. Don't worry."

Why did the idiot doctor, who was Persian, Mahnaz, let the operation go on as scheduled? he wondered out loud.

"I have the same question," I said. "Okay. I will call you later."

I got off the phone, still crying, walking, and talking to myself.

At last, Mother came to. She asked, "Where is the bag they said they would attach to me?"

I said, "Mother, they did not do any operation. Your heart failed."

The friend of my brother, a surgeon who mother liked, was there. He looked into my mother's eyes and said, "She is leaving us. She is in a coma."

That's when I ran and called my uncle, crying. The ICU staff was great. Everyone did a great job. My brother from San Diego, Farhad, came, and we all had some shifts with her (I still have the schedule). But he had to leave and go back to work. We all did our share of taking care of her.

I remember that, when she came out of the coma, she would say, "Go and call Bijan" (her brother) "from the yard" (meaning the hospital corridor). But she meant for us to call Farhad, my brother. She was hallucinating.

She once said of the hospital, "This is the house of Haji's Agha Tehrani" (her uncle and a famous and rich man in the bazaar of Tehran who owned mosques).

I said, "No, Mother. This is the hospital."

She insisted I take her to the bathroom with all the tubes attached to her just so she could fart. And when I asked why she wouldn't fart in her bed, she said, "We have prestige! And this is Haj agha Tehrani's house."

After her doctors stopped her medication, she returned to normal and did not remember a word of what had happened. The night before she was released, I was called by her nurse to come over because the woman next to her was acting weird and scaring her. My mother did not speak much English and, not understanding what the woman was saying, would get scared. I ran in the middle of the night and took my car to the hospital. I was exhausted, depressed, and out of motivation physically and emotionally. I hit a car parked in the hospital parking lot; got out of my car to look; and, seeing that nothing had happened, parked my car and ran fast to my mother's rescue.

She was sitting in her bed and scared. The doctors had given her medications, and I said, "I will stay here and take care of you."

My mother said, "One of the nurses wants to kill me."

I assured her I would stay with her. I had to sit in one of those narrow chairs lined up with a division between each of them. There was no way to sleep, but I stayed to assure her I was there.

In the morning, I went home and was called to return as my mother was being released. My brother and his wife came over to my house in Alexandria to get Mother settled in my house. As we were busy making her bed, a loud knock was on the door.

I opened the door said, "Yes?" OMG there were two policemen standing at my door. I said, "What?"

They said, "You did a hit-and-run in the hospital's parking lot, and we need to take you to the station."

I looked around and said, "But my mother is sick, and we just came back from the hospital. What do you suggest I do?"

They said, "We saw you on our camera."

I looked around, and my brother said, "You have to go. We'll take Mother to our house."

One thing after the other, bad stuff was happening. My nerves were broken. I started crying and followed the policeman. At the station, I explained my situation again and again, and I got a fine of $1,000 dollars, and my record went bad. I started drinking and smoking. I remembered that, when I'd stopped smoking, I'd been told that, if something really bad were to happen, I might start again. I had quit through hypnotism.

That was when I rented an apartment a floor above me with Mother's money, and she stayed there, visited by my uncle and her friends. She would cook her delicious food, and my friend Mary would go and eat fish and rice and vegetables cooked Iranian style. I had met this guy, Mehrdad, who would later become my last husband and who unfortunately has the same name as my sister's husband. I divorced him one year after our marriage.

Mother cooked for us, or we would bring cake for her birthday and would act normal. Sometimes she would go to my other brother's in San Diego, and sometimes she'd stay with me or my brother in Reston in a different house. They bought a house in Ashburn, and their son, Shaahin, was growing and would help too.

He had OCD, and we did not know about this disease. That was another problem for them to endure. I love him and pray that a cure comes for that. That was another "what-would-people-say" matter in my brother and his wife's eyes. I hate that aberoo stuff. It ruins so many people. So many girls are killed in any religion for dating a boy and causing the family's aberroo or prestige to go down. It's a logic for illiterate, narrow-minded people.

Continuing Mother's story, she left for Iran. And there were my uncle Daee Farhang, a heart physician; Soraya Joon, his wife; and my sister, Shahla, and her family. But they also had two full-time nurses to take care of Mother. Here, on the other hand, there were three of us—me, Farzad, and Roya—and, in San Diego, Farhad and his wife, Fari, with no nurses helping us and all of us with our own full-time jobs. I had to call and ask how she was doing, and the no-good husband of my sister would use any occasion to harass me and verbally abuse me.

I married Mehrdad, with a prenuptial arrangement, the guy who I had been dating. He was a professor at SEU University, and my sister's husband's name was Mehrdad too. I hated her husband so much that, in the beginning, I asked my Mehrdad if I could call him something else. "How about Houshang?" he suggested. We laughed; that was my uncle's name.

Once I called to check on Mother, and my sister's husband answered the phone and no one was home. "There is a God on my side," he said. "Now you have to hug your husband and say Mehrdad Joon" (his name followed by *dear*). I hung up quickly every time he answered. I told my husband of a year about my brother-in-law's harassment. We lived in a townhouse in Falls Church, Virginia.

Mother returned from Iran, and when she saw that my new husband and I slept in separate bedrooms, she said, "You should divorce him and come to Iran and take care of me."

I said, "What about my son? I can divorce my husband, but I won't come to Iran because my son is here."

I would later be going through a nasty divorce with him and would be unable to take care of Mother. My brothers decided at last that it was better if she went back to Iran. There were more people around her—my sister and her family and other relatives—and some doctors, like my uncle.

When we put mother on the plane, she could hardly walk and was in a wheelchair. I knew this was the last time I would see her. I wanted to run back and rush onto the plane, but the hostesses would not let me. I returned to a broken home and to the last courses I needed to complete to get my MBA.

Death of Mother, Thanksgiving Day 2001

I made a decision. I would get my degree, and then I would see my son for maybe the last time for a long time. I would go to Iran and take care of Mother. It was Thanksgiving, and we all went to San Diego. My son was there with a friend, and so were my brother and his wife, Fari, and their son Ardeshir, as well as Mehrdad, my husband. We celebrated Thanksgiving, and we had a great time. Then Babak and my then husband and I left to return to LA and each fly back. I said, "I feel happy now being with you, Babak Joon." I was thinking that maybe I wouldn't see him for a year when I went to Iran, but I remembered our visits were always close to that far apart anyways.

I asked to stop the car so I could go to the bathroom. Then I heard a noise. It was Mehrdad's cell phone, which he'd left in the trunk. We opened the trunk of the car and saw it was my brother telling us to return.

"What happened?" I asked.

He said, "They called from Tehran and said that your mother died. Your brother is calling and asking us to head back."

The news hit me hard. I started crying. I could not walk to the bathroom. It felt like a mile to me to get there.

We returned immediately, and I hugged Farhad, and we both cried. It reminded us of when Father died. Farhad and I had been together that New Year's day and had heard the news of my father's death together. Farhad started playing a song, "How Fragile We Are." He, his wife, and son, along with Babak, Mehrdad, and I sat there brokenhearted.

Family called, and everyone came over the next day. Babak had to go back to school. I kissed him and said my goodbyes, and he returned to school.

That was a Thanksgiving in November that I will never forget, as I went from being so happy, having spent my first Thanksgiving with my son to, hours later, so miserable. It was November 2001. I did not tell him of the plan I had to go to Iran in December.

Mother's death hit me and all of us hard. As much as you expect it, when it happens, it's very hard. She was only seventy-two years old and had a hard life, devoted to her children.

Up to this day, I have not seen my mother's grave. For that matter, I have not seen my grandmother Zinat Joon's grave either. I heard this stupid regime of Iran has demolished many people's graves. My grandma had a double grave with my grandpa in Shahabdilazim, a holy place for Muslims to visit. Then they demolished his grave and gave my grandma another grave close to that location, with the help of my Uncle Houshang. But later, even that was demolished. Now I have pictures of their graves, my mother's and my grandma's. On my last visit to Iran twenty-five years ago, I did visit my father's grave. But then after my grandma died, my mother came to the United States with cancer, and since then, we were busy with her. Then when I decided to go to Iran, my mother died. I have no desire to return to Iran, especially with the mandatory hijab rule. And because I have so publicly expressed my hatred for the regime in Iran, I might be arrested in the airport. So far, I have not seen either grave. Maybe one day, when the mandatory hijab rule is removed to honor women's liberation I will go and visit all. May God bless their souls.

CHAPTER 41

JOBS I HELD IN MY LIFE: LITTLE ODD JOBS BETWEEN JOBS, 1974–2016

Throughout my life, since graduation from Purdue University until I got two more master's degrees in America, I have worked constantly—mostly in the computer field and or teaching positions. My first job was at Earlham College as a salad girl in 1970. Then I went to Purdue. There I had odd jobs, like babysitter and Avon lady selling cosmetics. Then I graduated with a degree in computer sciences and returned to Iran.

In Iran I worked for IBM, a planning and budget organization, the Cultural Affairs of the King's Court, and IEI (Iran Electronics Industry), all in the capacity of a computer specialist / programmer. Languages like Fortran, system 3, and DATATRIEVE were what I used there, as well as systems like IBM and digital.

Then the revolution happened, and I moved to Switzerland. There, I was working as a programmer for a Greek company and then at a digital company. After that, I returned to the United States. Several computer languages were used at those jobs.

In the United States, I had any job you could think of. I was a contractor as a computer specialist, but between jobs, I accepted any jobs available—from temporary to long-term positions. I was constantly in survival mode. I started with CSC and got my work permit and green card through that company. Then I landed a job in the Treasury Department and, after that, worked at U.S. Mint, which makes coins in the United States. There I was primarily using Fortran, COBOL, and IDMS. Then I worked as a programmer and contractor in the Education

Department, running Cobol batch jobs for student loans. The figures coming out of that batch job were used by the president at the time, President Bill Clinton, in his speeches. It was too much responsibility, and sometimes I had a pager with me and would get a call at 2:30 a.m. We had to debug the program right there and then. No cell phones, Skype, or FaceTime. We were just given an error number, and I had to suggest ways to debug the program and fast. The pressure was high. Everyday at work was like taking a test, a hard exam.

I was working and working and would rest when my son was visiting me. Then I would be happy, and I'd be sad again after a week when he would leave and I would return to working and working. No one was taking care of me. And the situation in Iran was getting worse and worse, specially for Baha'is. I was worried for my son because he was half Baha'i. He said he didn't believe in anything of the Baha'i faith, but his last name would make it always dangerous for him around the Khomeini/Khamenei regime in Iran.

I also had jobs between contracting jobs. I was a bank teller, a Costco food tester, a saleswoman at a store called Garfinckel's, a Lord & Taylor dress seller, an ESL teacher, and an Excel and access teacher to soldiers at Fort Myer next to Arlington Cemetery. I was an adjunct at NOVA (Northern Virginia Community College) too. I was a realtor at a company after I passed the realtor's exam and got my certificate. I took courses in loan officer jobs and got degrees and certificates in any job I could find to survive and bring my son over to visit me every year. I had telemarking jobs, sitting in huge rooms where hundreds of us would call people to give them good deals on their telephone service. Most of the time, people would hang up on us. I would take a metro to go to Washington, DC.

I also worked as a hospital registration agent. I lost that job since my brother and his wife decided to ask their son Shaahin to come and live with me. He would come home late and sometimes drunk. He had OCD, and I tried to be nice to him. But being up at nights and always worrying about him cost me that job. I cannot imagine how my brother and his wife managed all those years raising him. They must have lots of patience. The thing is, Shaahin is so nice at one time and a different person at another time, and it's not his fault; it's the OCD disease.

For each job, I have memories to tell—how I was treated as a well-paid computer programmer compared to my treatment as a clerk in the food-tasting department of Costco. But my system was used to being a yo-yo—sometimes up, sometimes down, sometimes different, and sometimes ordinary.

One of my last jobs in Washington, DC, was as a grocery store owner for Persians. It was called Asia Market, and I added the name "Mehr" (meaning kindness) to it. I just heard that not many women were in economic positions, and this store was going bankrupt, so I bought it. It was the hardest job for a woman all alone to do. I ran Asia Market as a woman alone. No other Persian store was run by a woman in the Metropolitan area at that time. I was the sole owner, there and then, although the store's rental lease stayed in the last owner's name, as the landlord of that store, on Route 7 of Falls Church, refused to put a woman's name on the contract. That was in 1997/98 in Virginia. My purpose was to show that women could manage economic businesses, and I did that for a year. My brother said he has seen men getting old fast running a supermarket, and he was right. It was not easy, especially as I was doing it alone.

I also helped teach in a Farsi school for children in DC. That was run by a family for children of political men and women fighting against the regime of Iran. But that happened when I was cured from my despair over being near children. I went from being away from kids to trying to be close to children as therapy.

I also, for a short while, was teaching Farsi to some Americans. One in particular was a handsome blue-eyed kid of nineteen years old, and he was so good at Farsi that he was studying Rumi and poetry. That office was in Maryland.

The best jobs I had money-wise were during the conversion of dates when the year turned from 1999 to 2000. So many programs were supposed to be changed and coding updated to prepare for Y2K. Job hunters were giving a prize to whoever would introduce me to the companies in need of making changes in their systems. Humans get prepared when the time comes for a change. No one predicts changes, though every day of life is a constant change. I worked with several companies as a contractor to change their codes, but those jobs were over in two years. I also had a small job as a driver for Auto zone, a company that sells parts for cars, and I would deliver them.

I got my MBA in information technology in Washington, DC, at a university called Southeastern University. My one-year marriage was in that time. I graduated in 2000 and left DC for good in 2004. I'll write that part of my story later. This chapter is just about the jobs I held in my life.

Even when I visited Iran for the last time in 1992, I was working as an Excel/Access programmer. Memories of that job are unusual ones, as we were paid in cash in a brown bag. I would come home and empty all the cash on my bed. Once, the government guards came to check and see whether we had any sign saying, "Hijabs are mandatory" in our office. They saw none and closed that office for four weeks, punishing us. That day, I had tested a nail polish remover in a store, and my thumb did not have any nail polish on it. I held the book in my hand so that only my thumb would show. The guards looked at me and saw no makeup and no nail polish, so they passed me by, but the secretary had some mascara on, and she was arrested. At that time, the guards were way stricter. A little hair shown below the scarf, lipstick, nail polish, and makeup were forbidden. One would get arrested. Wearing no socks was also a crime.

This was a religion we never heard of, as Islam was practiced always in Iran before the revolution, and these rules after the revolution were made up. The beginning of the revolution was a time during which many were arrested, killed, and imprisoned. Everybody's fault was being with the Shah; sometimes just breathing under the Shah's regime was a fault in the guard's eyes. We made a sign and wrote, "Sisters, Hijab is Mandatory," and put it next to the bathroom. We were closed for a month. I was mainly there to see my grandma, as the last time I would spend with her, and visit my father's grave. But even during that time, I was working.

More jobs

When I moved to California, I held a number of jobs. I worked in Lompoc in an auto store as a driver and at Allan Hancock College as a part-time computer programmer. I was a substitute teacher for Lompoc schools. Then as a teacher, I was a helper for Maple High School, which had students who were either pregnant or used drugs or were just different. I was a private math tutor too and loved my students. They all improved.

Then I was approached by a friend's friend about a job in Monterey as a Farsi teacher for soldiers in America. It was at Defense Language Institute (DLI), and all languages—among them Chinese, Vietnamese, Hebrew, Arabic, and Russian—were taught. It was a great base overlooking the ocean. All my coworkers were Persian, and the work wasn't easy. I was not totally Persian anymore, but DLI liked to hire those who know less English because they spoke the language authentic. I was really miserable there. I quit and retired before the trouble grew and moved to Camarillo an hour away from Santa Barbara.

As you can guess, I had different résumés. In order to not be labeled as overqualified, I would omit some experiences depending on the job I was aiming for.

I may look for a part-time job next year. But this is the first year that I am without a job, and I feel I deserve it, as I've worked constantly all my life. My job now is writing this book. I do deserve my retirement. However, after writing this book, I might go for a part time job. Who knows?

The job I always wanted to have was being a secretary. My mother did not let me choose that field. She said, "You need to be the boss, not the secretary." But my dream was to be the secretary for a CEO of a big organization. At the moment, I am the secretary of our little book club where I live, a club with twelve members, all women. It is called Dotti's Book Club. I love this honorary job. All the members love what I do for the club. At last I did it my way.

I've had different short-term jobs, the longest for eight years, as well as different degrees. I earned an MBA in information technology. I also hold a master's degree in education from Chapman University and lots of certificates. I've had different cars and houses. Nothing was to stay. Everything was temporary—from jobs to houses to cars.

Visiting my son was always temporary too. Every step of my life was temporary. I was in love with telephone because that was how I could contact my son. I was angry with happy people who had their families close to them. No one understood me. All would say, "Wait till he grows up. Wait till he graduates from school. Wait till he gets married. Wait till he has children." I am waiting and waiting. The only permanent part of my life has been waiting to have a good and normal relationship with my son. I have not had a full Christmas, Thanksgiving, or birthday with him yet. I have one- to two-hour visits. He thinks that is normal. In the words of Persian singer Marzieh, my heart says, "I am so hurt, so neglected it's unbearable. What should I say when my crazy heart longs for you and longs for you? One day, I got fed up and took my heart out of my chest and stepped on it. Under my foot, my heart was murmuring, 'I long for you.'"

CHAPTER 42

LIVING IN RESTON, 2003–2005: A WOMAN AND THE CHALLENGES IN HER LIFE

I once heard that, "Behind a woman's back, two kinds of men talk—one you don't sleep with and one you don't sleep with anymore."

Being young and pretty with a good figure and sociable and easy to laugh when you feel like it, mixed with occasional drinking and divorce make the perfect recipe for hungry men to do their best to catch you. I was only twenty-seven when I got divorced. I had all the characteristic some men with small brains were looking for in a woman who is approachable.

After the stupid marriage to and divorce from my last husband of a year (from 2001 to 2002), I moved to Reston and brought my furniture, which was in storage. So far, everything I had done was wrong . I read somewhere, "The difference between fiction and reality is that fiction has to make sense." So if my real life does not make sense, then wait to read my next book, which will be fiction. Maybe that one will.

One New Year in 2003, Babak came to Reston with his girlfriend Claudia. That was the only Persian New Year I ever spent with him. We were only a couple of hours late, but it was a great improvement as to waiting for thirty or so years. We went to a party at Shahin and Saeed's house, the couple who let me stay at their house after I'd had disagreements with Mehrdad, my last husband. Babak and Claudia and all the kids from the family were together, and it felt good and normal again. But they left after two days, and I was alone in Reston.

My house was on the second floor. I felt dizzy one day as I woke up and took a shower. I felt not normal. Later, we found out that my furnace was so old and rotten that I was getting carbon monoxide poisoning. I changed it and tried to sell that house. I made some money on the sale, but I was missing Babak so much that I decided to move to California.

Going to California, 2005

I discussed my idea of moving to California to be closer to my son with a colleague of years ago, Dick Holmberg. He said he wanted to drive to California too, and he would help me go there. It was a huge step. I had to pack all my belongings in a large yellow truck from either Penske or Budget and also haul my car at the back of that truck. God forbid if you went by mistake to a narrow street and needed to back up.

Dick Goldberg looked just like my paternal grandfather, and I would tease him. He was an IDMS/COBOL programmer and years older than me. I felt comfortable with him. We started our trip and said goodbye to all our relatives and those who helped me and also all the bad memories I had in the DC Metropolitan Area. The only person I really missed was Mary, my friend and neighbor in Alexandria. She was the one who rescued my furniture when Mehrdad was encouraging me to throw everything away and go live with him and marry him. She gave them all back to me. In fact this secretary that I am using now to write my story on is one of the items rescued by Mary, and it's still with me.

We took Route 10 and passed a number of states on our way. I liked Louisiana and all its rivers; I liked every state. Texas was the largest and longest to drive through. On the way saw Kami, my mother's photographer and a friend of my sister and her husband's and mine. We would only stop for an hour for lunch or at nights to sleep in a motel. I drove part of the way and thought about how being a truck driver was the only thing I had not done before. And now here I was.

We got to Arizona, and it was raining. I'd always wanted to see the Arizona sky and its beautiful stars but could not. I still hope to drive there and see it, but we had a long way ahead of us.

Before leaving, I'd talked to my cousin Shahram, who lived near Lompoc in a city called Orcutt and asked if I could come and stay with them for a while until I found myself a place. Shahram and his wife, Claudia, along with his children, Mina, Kiana, Tanya, and Christina, were living in a three-bedroom house with a pool, and he was working for Boeing. He'd worked for Boeing with my brother in San Diego before, and now he'd moved to this part of California.

We parked the big car with my Honda attached to it, and Dick Holmberg and I got out the car. They were all outside looking at us with open mouths. I slept with Kiana and Tanya in one room; Mina was in another room; and Shahram and Claudia and their youngest daughter, Christina, were in the master bedroom. Dick Holmberg left in a few days.

I started looking for a job and landed one at an auto parts store as a driver. I had to wear a red shirt and black trousers as a uniform. My uncle Houshang, Shahram's father, came to visit and saw me wearing that every day. I was ashamed to tell him about my real job, as I knew his mentality. He asked me one day, "Why do you wear these ugly clothes to work? Why don't you wear different clothes and have makeup on?"

I just smiled and said, "Because its comfortable, Daee Joon."

He loved parrots and fishing, and I did go with him to some events or meat swaps. I put all my furniture in Shahram's garage for a while. Later, I moved to Lompoc. I rented a room in a friend of Claudia's house in Lompoc and again put my furniture in a section of her garage.

I will always be thankful to Shahram and Claudia.

At last, I landed a job at Allan Hancock College as a part-time computer programmer. I moved out of that house to a one-bedroom apartment in Lompoc. Farhad my brother and Farnaz and their son, Ardeshir, and Shahla my sister and my cousin Nahid all came to visit me in that condo. My brother got me some groceries, knowing my job paid me very little. And after that, all disappeared, and I would only see them once a year on Persian New Year and my son too. That once a year was so important to me, as the occasions to see my son were few and precious. That was cut off later, and it really hurt my heart. I will explain in greater detail later how, after years and years of silence, I broke my silence about my sister's husband's behavior to me, and the whole family cut me off.

If I had a sweet memory in Lompoc, it was of the time I taught math to high school kids. The first day, they would be indifferent. But after some visits, I would see the excitement in their eyes, as they solved some problems and started learning. Their parents got excited, as they got good grades. I was fulfilled.

CHAPTER 43

MY POLITICAL LIFE, 1994–1998

1. Mujahideen, NCR Cheriks, and the National Front

I first came to know about this political group as opposition to the regime of mullahs in Iran when my brother came to Iran after the revolution and my divorce. That was in 1979. I was planning to go to a part of town in Tehran that was blocked to cars. A friend of my brother's, Hamid, gave me a ride on his motorcycle, and I ran my errands in downtown Tehran. To thank him, I asked, "How much do I owe you?"

He said, "I don't want money. But if you want, you can give a donation to the Mujahideen."

"How?" I asked.

He said, "If you give me the money, I will give it to them."

I asked, "Are they against this regime?"

"Yes," he told me.

The head of that organization was called Masood Rajavi, and only thing I knew about him was that he'd married the daughter-in-law of Mr. Nabavi, a top manager of the education department working for my aunt as secretary of education. Masood's wife was called Ashraf. At the time, I knew nothing about her, except that she was the daughter-in-law of Mr. Nabavi. This Ashraf was adored by the Mujahideen of Iran.

I gave him a little money, and months later, I heard that he was killed being with the Mujahideen of Iran.

Years passed, and one day as I was sitting in my condo in Alexandria, Virginia, around 1986, a Mujahed girl knocked at my door, collecting money for the organization. Her name was Mojgan. As she was sitting there, someone knocked at the door. She turned her head and saw the picture that my mother had on that desk with my sister and her family. She said, "OMG. Is that Shahla? And Mehrdad?"

I said yes. Shahla was my sister.

"I am the cousin of her husband, Mehrdad," she told me.

She was family in a way, and I asked more about her. She explained that she was so absorbed in the Mujahideen that she is leaving for Iraq to join them, along with her husband Saeed too. At that time, Iran and Iraq were in a war with each other, and the Mujahideen base was in Iraq.

Two things about them absorbed me, or maybe three. One was that, in that group, women were more important than men. The elected president was a woman called Maryam, and Masood was her second husband. Second was the fact that they were all separated from their children and spouses and family. I hated that, but I also felt like someone here understood what it meant to be separated from your child, and I felt comfortable around them. The last thing was having Jebheh Melli and Mosaddegh and his grandchild, Mr. Hedayat Matin Daftari, as part of the organization at that time.

I did not like that they wore hijabs as part of their uniform. Nor did I like the fact that there were strange rules, like those on a military base. I liked that they had demonstrations against the regime of mullahs in Iran. I got to know some of them and found out there was lots of news related to the organization about which the general public of Iranians had no idea.

I started talking to a Persian radio station in LA with a reporter called Mr. Alireza Meybodi. I'd gotten to know him through Mr. Toufighee, who used to cover the news in camping(ordoo) in the Iranian seaside. It was the same radio station my mother was always listening to. I would give the reports that this reporter and all of them were hiding from people. I would also ask them to come to demonstrations, and that was how I started listening to the radio station my mother used to hear every day. I would mention every time that I was not part of the Mujahideen and had very little in common with them. But the announcer, Mr. Meybodi, who was anti-Islam and anti-Mujahideen was just thinking of how to make his program juicier and get more listeners. It's like when you hear Fox News and CNN and how differently they interpret some of the news but way worse.

This group, the Mujahideen of Iran, then became a council called NCR, and many different Iranian opposition political groups joined them—among them the nationalists, the leftists, and the Cheriks. But in reality the Mujahideen was it, and the rest had no real power.

I did not stay in contact with the organization long, and it's been years and years that I've had no news from them—especially since I left Washington, DC, more than seventeen years ago and started living in California.

There was an incident that made me dislike the organization. I knew through Mojgan and others, like Shahnaz, a Cherik living in the DC area, that the organization had a huge house in a good part of Virginia. I went there to deliver a message via a letter. I took the letter to a Mujahed girl called Sona from her sister, saying her mother was dying and she should call her. She did not open the letter and threw it in a wastebasket. The Mujahideen promoted heroic acts and acts like this too. You had to be totally devoted and forget your family and only fight against the regime of Iran. That was not so human to me, and I hated that aspect of the group. To me, that was torturing yourself, not the enemy. But their logic was that, if they stayed in contact with their families, then the regime would take their family members hostage in order to capture them. Politics are complicated and dirty.

I did go to Paris once, following my brother. I was worried about his whereabouts and wanted to protect him, not knowing what this group was really about. If I had a second life, I would have never done that. He never understood why I was there. A great Persian poet says, "I wish I had two lives, one to gather experiences and another to use those experiences."

They even took a picture of me, and the waiters serving us dinner were top members of the Mujahideen. I did not notice and my brother pointed that out. But they had no base with the majority of people.

I saw Maryam Rajavi, the president, and lots of their top people but not Masood Rajavi himself. Later, Marzieh, a very famous singer in Iran and a friend of my aunt and family, joined them too. I did and still do like Mr. Matin Daftari and his wife, Maryam, the head of the National Front the best. I could identify with them. I can identify with Reza Pahlavi, the son of the late Shah of Iran too. But he was not holding any demonstrations then. I am not too much of an Iranian after living for forty-five years in the United States altogether, from my student time till now, but I hope the regime of Iran changes ASAP.

2. Cheriks: Political life

I met Shahnaz as a hairdresser. When I said I like Bakhtiar as a nationalist figure, she said, "You do not know what you're talking about."

As Moe was teaching me what the leftists believed in and Shahnaz was once a student of Moe under Iran's confederation of Iranian students, she was trying to teach me the other side of the leftist group called Cherikhaye Fadayee Khalghe Iran. The group was under the supervision of Mehdi Saamea and Zinat Mir Hashemi, leaders and publishers of the publication *Navbarde Khalgh*, working parallel with the Mujahideen. I was learning from both sides what a leftist believes. Moe was against the Mujahideen, and Shahnaz was pro.

At one point, Shahnaz had a hysterectomy and asked another guy and me to help her make the Persian New Year's card of Cheriks in the DC area and beyond. I went with this guy to a Kinko's store and took a picture from a book. The guy at the counter and the manager was called Toni. He said we couldn't make three hundred copies of that picture, since it had a copyright. The guy with me—I'll call him Asad because I can see his face in my memory but have forgotten his name—said, "Okay, Toni. Can I have just one picture, and we'll leave?"

Toni said, "Okay."

Then Asad and I left and sat in our car. He had a plan. He said he'd heard that Toni was going to lunch soon. He had a Cherik brain all right. After we saw Toni leaving the store for lunch, we walked in, and Asad asked for three copies showing them only the one copy of the picture. Remember, this was at the time of no cell phones and no Google. So since what we'd presented was a copy, the clerk accepted.

But after 130 copies had been printed, all got ruined, and the clerk threw all of them away in a basket. He started copying again, and we were worried Toni would come back soon. At last we got the copies, and as we were getting ready to pay, Toni returned from lunch and stood right next to that wastebasket. We were worried that, if he saw 130 copies of that picture, he would stop us. But our copies were in a bag, and he could not see what we had inside. Also, he did not see the basket.

We ran as fast as we could out of the store. Since then, every time we would say Toni, we would laugh. That year I had a hand in making the New Year's cards of the Cheriks. Is that a crime? I did not even believe in that group, but I had fun doing that. Again, don't ask for logic in the real events of life. Logic is just for fictions. In between the sorrows of life and fighting for the freedom of people there is laughter too.

I was most active in 1994, trying to help make a women's club. We visited senators asking for the liberation of Iran and also the liberation of women due to mandatory hijab rules in the brutal anti-human rights regime of Iran. The senators told us, "We give ten minutes time to each group, and your group talked against the regime in Iran for the entire ten minutes. But other groups speak against the Mujahideen for eight minutes and against the regime of Iran for two minutes."

I felt the Persian radio stations were doing the same. It isn't easy for Persians to come together. They don't fight against the common enemy, as they'd rather fight against the closest idea to themselves—as it is with religion. Everyone likes Buddha, but the other religions that all believe in one God are constantly fighting with each other, trying to proving which one is correct!

3. Moe the leftist and pro-confederation, 1986–1990

I also asked Moe about the leftist ideology. He was a teacher in that way and very active in the confederation. He was once the teacher of Shahnaz. Once, in a bus in Turkey, he just showed his old driver's license and was rescued as an American.

So he told me a lot about the philosophy of Marx and Trotsky while we were walking in parks or going here and there. Gradually, he got more serious and was asking for my hand. But his daughter disagreed with our union, and I did not feel at all like starting a relation on that basis was a good idea. So I stayed away. Later on, I heard he had cancer. I felt sorry for him and went to visit him.

He had his last cigarette and a glass of wine with me, and he had a needle in his neck. I knew that, when the doctors did that, it meant he was in the last stages of cancer. After that, I heard he was moved to a hospital and died there.

When I heard that he was in the hospital, I asked my then husband Mehrdad if I could go and see him and he said no. I would not do the same. I would let my husband go see a dying friend on his deathbed.

I got the news of Moe's death the night before my hysterectomy operation around the year 2000 among the many calls I received that night wishing me well for my operation. I cancelled the operation and postponed it for later—without telling anyone when it was scheduled so I wouldn't get any calls the night before. That I'll explain more in the section where I write about my divorce from my last husband—another parallel event in life and another item in the bowl of changes of my life.

The more I learned about the leftists, the more I respected a simple religious person because he or she would believe in God and was afraid of wrongdoing, but the leftist did not and were not. It seemed to me that they were waiting for the last person in all the remote places on earth to become "aware" and also learn about the leftists. Then they could prove their theories. Also I did not like their way of respecting women and giving them freedom because it was all to the men's advantage.

Real equality and freedom have not yet been given to women by any group, in my opinion. When the laws in all the offices and organizations have changed to accommodate the differences in the bodies of men and women and their functionalities, having equal rights and opportunities in mind, then real equality will be given to women. Again, I would like to see a demand for having periods, pregnancies, breastfeeding, and child birth considered in the laws of every organization. That would be a real struggle for the equality of men and women.

4. National Front (Mosaddegh) political life, 1992–1995

Here, I would like to explain about Mr. Matin Daftari, the leader of the National Front, and his wife. The time I met that couple was in Washington, DC. I was running toward them to see the grandchild of Mosaddegh, and they were running toward me seeing me as grandchild of Fakhr Afagh Parsay. Go figure. Also, they separated themselves from the Mujahideen years and years ago. To write this part, I called him in London and talked to him on the phone today, April 2020, after fifteen years.

Mr. Matin Daftari is the grandchild of Mosaddegh, someone my father would have loved to meet. He was the son of Mosaddegh's daughter, Mansoureh Khanum, and Mr. Ahmad Matin Daftari. The day I met them, I decided to be around them since they were heading a party called Jebheh Melli, National Democratic Front (Iran), and that meant any nationalist with any opinion or political preference would be accepted, as it was a national front. I was also drawn to them because of the fact that he had the best publication, called *Azadi* (*Freedom*). In addition, Maryam Matin Daftari (Khajeh Nouri), his wife, was pro-women's liberation movement. As this was the purpose of my life (and, for that matter, had been my grandmother Mrs. Fakhr Afagh Parsay's purpose in life), we had many common grounds. I felt more comfortable accepting the Mujahideen with the mandatory hijab as their uniform, knowing this woman was fighting too and was without a hijab. I went to their demonstrations against the regime of mullahs in Iran. I can say that no other organization was as active as these people, and if someone hated the regime of Iran, she or he had to go to demonstrations that these people held. I talked to this couple a lot. They once even came to Washington and my house in Falls Church, when I was living with Mehrdad, my short-term last husband. I am glad I could see them.

I just called Mr. Matin Daftari in London, in these corona virus days, and asked him, "What are your memories of Mosaddegh?"

And he said, "Mosaddegh, my grandfather, and Mr. Ali Akbar Daftari, my uncle, were arrested by Reza Shah for plotting against the government of Iran at that time." His uncle was sent to prison and Mosaddegh was exiled to Birjand in a house—until a good friend of Mohammad Reza Shah's from his school in Switzerland, Ernest Peron, got sick. At that time, Mohammad Reza Shah was the prince and not the shah. When he finished school in Switzerland, he brought his best friend, Ernest Peron, to Iran. This Swiss guy lived in the court of Iran. Once Peron got sick, Dr. Gholamhossain Mosaddegh, son of Mosaddegh cured him.

When Peron was released from the hospital, he asked the doctor, "I am so thankful to you. What can I do for you?"

Dr. Ghalmhossain Mosaddegh said, "Can you please talk to your friend, Prince Mohammad Reza Pahlavi, and ask him to release my father, Mosaddegh, from house arrest?"

Peron did his part, and Prince Mohammad Reza at that time arranged a deal so that Mosaddegh was released from Birjand to go to his own property in Ahmad Abad and live there. When Reza Shah was toppled and forced to leave Iran, his son Mohammad Reza Shah set Mosaddegh free.

Per Dr. Hedayat Matin Daftari, "When the shah of Iran was changed, the country became a democracy from dictatorship. Mosaddegh became an auditor in Khorasan province, north of Iran."

The rest is history—how Mosaddegh nationalized the oil, so that it was no longer owned by the British but was now Iranian owned, with the Shah and also how he revolted against the Shah but wanted the monarchy but with some conditions. I leave the rest to be googled by readers.

Among other personal memories Mr. Matin Daftari told me was that Mosaddegh bought him a donkey and loved all his grandkids and that they always visited him in Ahmad Abad. He also said that he married Mrs. Maryam Khajeh Nouri, a relative, and both, side by side, were fighting for freedom of Iran to this day.

He told me too that his mother had died when flying from Mashhad, a holy city in Iran, to Tehran. The plane hit a mountain and crashed when the specialist and the religious people in the control tower were fighting over control. Events like this—and the many other deaths due to the stupidity of the regime of Iran after the revolution—are referred to by the opposition to the regime as the side crimes of the regime, as opposed to its direct crimes.

Mr. and Mrs. Matin Daftari have written many books and magazines and published articles here and there. I hope they see the day that Iran is freed from the fake religious regime of Iran. They left the Mujahideen years and years ago, as they found out that the Mujahideen of Iran only accepted themselves and no one else. The Mujahideen do have their own heroic acts, and one can find out about them by googling.

At one point, Mr. Matin Daftari sent me a piece of a magazine that was about a poem my father composed. On the page that my father's poetry was printed, it explains that his job was the head of City Hall Court in Abadan and his poem follows. My father really liked Mosaddegh and was a good poet too. I cannot translate it. I was not born yet, and there was no way I could know about the events that led to his writing of the poem unless he had written his memoires too. Thanks to Mr. Hedayat Matin Daftari, the grandson of Mosaddegh, for sending me that.

I came into this world a couple of months after this poem was recited by my father, Farrokh Pour Parsay. I include a picture of my parents while my mother was pregnant with me.

We each build an opinion about a political figure depending on how much information is available to us, plus how much our own belief system accepts the ideas espoused by that figure. But in the end, we all want to have the best for our fellowmen.

5. Family political life: My aunt and grandparents

While I am on this subject, I want to mention that the Dafartis' magazine, *Azadi*, was the one that published my article about the days when my aunt was captured. It was translated to English later, and I include that here. Also my book *Women and Rules of the Society* was printed in the *Nabarde Khalgh* magazine periodically, run by a leftist group headed by Zinat and Mehdi Samae.

CHAPTER 44

MY PUBLICATION, 2000

With thanks to Mr. Manuchehri and Mr. Simon Farsi, I'm able to include the English translation of the article I wrote for *Azadi*:

This piece was originally written by Roya Parsay for the journal *Azadi* published by the Iranian National Democratic Front in spring 2000. The author starts by recording her recollections of the final days leading up to the execution of her aunt Farrokh-Ru Parsay, the first female Minister ever to be appointed in Iran.

Born to parents with a solid intellectual and journalistic background, Farrokh-Ru pursued her education career and then became involved in modern politics. During her parliamentary career she was instrumental in drafting a number of reform bills aimed at elevating the status of women in the society. During the course of her ministry, she was credited with the establishment of over 100 new schools in Iran, training and employing an unprecedented number of women as schoolteachers and introducing the "free nourishment" program aimed at distributing free food to primary and secondary students across the country.

As an attachment to the main article, the author encloses biographies of Farrokh-Ru Parsay, her mother Fakhr-Afaq Parsay and her father Farrokh-Din Parsay.

Farrokh-Ru Parsay was first entered the Majlis (Parliament) in 1962. In the summer of 1964 she was appointed as a Minister by then Prime Minister—Amir Abbas Hoveyda. Farrokh-Ru Parsay served in the Cabinet up until the resignation of Hoveyda in 1976.

Prior to her execution the authorities accused her of "being a Baha'i". This allegation was solidly rejected by both her and her family. This article reveals several interesting facts including:

Existence of personal diaries and notes that may provide more insight into the life and achievements of Farrokh-Ru Parsay

Records of her final interview from Prison which were later printed in Kayhan

Extracts from her defence statement which were also printed in Kayha, Sepehr Manuchehri, March 2002, Fakhr-Afaq Parsay and her daughter Farrokh-Ru Parsay (Extract from Roya Parsay's piece in *Azadi*, published by the Iranian National Democratic Front, 21 (spring 2000), 120–137. Edited and translated by Sepehr Manuchehri, March 2002)

I can recall vividly. After waking, I sat up instantly and wandered around the room to see where I was. Those days were indeed tremulous times. I had recently been separated from my husband and lived with my mother. The room was a little unfamiliar. I thought a little and remembered my dream. I'd had a dream about Maman-Baa'la, my grandmother Ms. Fakhr-Afaq Parsay. She always lived upstairs from us, so we called her Maman-Baa'la to distinguish her from our other grandmother. In the dream, she gave me a white envelope and said "I trust you with this. Carry on the tradition."

Maman had just passed away, and Ammih-jan[1] (Ms. Farrokh-Ru Parsay) was still in prison. Mum, my grandma, had witnessed the revolutionary guards arresting Ammih-jan. Upon leaving the house, she slammed a heavy blow to her chest, causing her to become ill instantly. She died a few days later at the house of Amoo-jan Farrokhzad, my uncle. At the time of burial, we were still bewildered. Ammih-jan and her husband (General Shirin Sokhan) were both kept in the parliamentary

---

[1] Meaning Dear Aunty, a popular expression among some Iranian families when addressing their close relatives.

prison. I recall that my cousin actually performed the burial prayers. We were dumbfounded by the various bits of revolutionary news and the arrest of Ammih-jan, who was the first female minister in the Royal Court. Khomeini had specifically stated that she would never be forgiven![2]

I rubbed my eyes and pondered a little.

Why me? I asked to myself. *As if I have no other problems, now Grandmother has picked on me.*

My two-year old son lived with my ex-husband's relatives. I was concerned about his well-being as they were Baha'is and this was an "Islamic revolution." Further more, I had been put on trial and dismissed from work for wearing black[3] and not obeying the Imam.

I constantly remembered Ammih-jan, who had come to visit us in the days prior to her arrest. I informed her about the recent interrogations at work, which went like this:

"Ms. Farrokh-Ru Parsay?"

"I am Roya Parsay. If you wish to see her, I can contact her for you."

"Where is she?"

"In her house."

"Anyway, why are you wearing black? Soon it will be her turn."

They referred me to another court with Ayatollah Rayshahri[4] as a judge for final determination.

I appealed to Ammih-jan. "Please leave this country."

She replied, "What have I done? What have I stolen? And what is their evidence?"

I said, "These people do not understand such things."

The determination court was held after the execution of Ammih-jan. Again, as I entered the court room, they referred to me as Farrokh-Ru, to which I objected.

---

[2] Reference to his Fatwa from Najaf dated summer 1962 soon after the appointment was made.

[3] The former prime minister of the Shah, the later Shahpour Bakhtyar, was now resident in Paris. He ran an opposition campaign from exile to oust the new regime. He had instructed that people wear black in public as a sign of protest against the gradual removal of their basic human rights. As a result the new regime was cracking down on men and women who wore black in the public.

[4] One of the influential clerics in the justice and prison systems.

The Judge asked, "Why have you ignored the imam's word?"

"Because as the Quran says, there is no force (in complying) to religion."[5]

"Yes, that is how the Baha'is put it."

"What does that mean? Besides, we are not Baha'is."

"They utter one half of the verse and neglect the other bits. What is the rest of this verse?"

"To tell you the truth, I can not recall. I read the English translation of the Quran by Yusuf Ali."

"Very well, Mrs. Farrokh-Ru Parsay."

"But I am Roya Parsay."

It was only here that I began to realize the full extent of each allegation against Ammih-jan. But Ammih-jan was married to a Tabatabai Sayyid and a descendant of Sadr-i Shirazi. Mum had read in the books that Mirza Masih Tehrani, who had murdered Gribadov, happened to be one our great grand parents.

Anyway, I described the dream to my mother and asked her permission to visit Ammih-jan in Prison. Her daughter Mahshid lived in Abadan and used to visit her each weekend. One week, in her absence, my mother paid a visit to the prison.

⌘

I recall the day when they finally succeeded in arresting her (on a previous occasion, the dumb guards actually caught Ammih-jan. She introduced herself as the sister of Ms. Parsay. They did not realize who she was and left her alone. Since that time, she lived in hiding at a friend's house). On that day, my mother had gone to my cousin Hamid's house. She did not return in time, so I called her. Not convinced by her tone, I went to Hamid's place immediately. Parked near the gate were two cars and several guards. I entered the house and saw Ammih-jan sitting on the couch.

Her son Hamid explained, "I even managed to send her out using the back door, but she promptly returned!"

---

[5] La' Ikrah'a fi-ldin

To the general who asked, "Where are you taking the lady?" the guards replied, "Now we will arrange a warrant for you to fully understand."

It was one of the most difficult periods of my life, resisting the temptation to slap the guard. I feared making life harder for Ammih-jan. Although it was evident that things would not get any worse, we hoped that, perhaps, this was simply a political maneuver and she could be released after detention. In reality, the period of arrests was now behind us, and only those who worked for SAVAK[6] or ministers whose departments committed murders were to be arrested. The veil had not yet been fully imposed and they needed victims.

I asked Ammih-jan, "Can I do anything?"

"Go and see if you can find Abbas."

"Is that all?"

"Yes. Go quickly."

I looked at her face one more time and left. Why didn't I hug her? She was concerned about my safety and knew that I would speak my mind and get involved in a brawl with the guards. I left in a fury.

We went to the former house of Lily Amir Arjomand in Niavaran.[7] This lad (Abbas) was previously unemployed and now was the personal bodyguard for (Ayatollah) Taliqani.[8]

If I had known this was he last time I would see her, I would never have left. Her face was so calm. She was tired of all the adventures and life on the run.

She said, "If they have arrested Hoveyda,[9] then they must arrest all of us who were ministers in his cabinet. Then I can testify that (Ayatollah) Beheshti[10] and

---

[6] Known as the secret service during the time of the Shah.

[7] A prestigious suburb in the North of Tehran. Arjomand's lavish residence had now been confiscated and used by the new leaders.

[8] An influential member of the New Revolutionary Council at the time.

[9] Amir Abbas Hoveyda, prime minister 1964–1977. Refer to "Khatirat-i Hoveyda" by Dr. Abbas Milani.

[10] Another influential member of the Revolutionary Council. He went on to head the Islamic Republic political party.

(Hojjat'ul Islam) Bahonar[11] were my employees. They must also be arrested, as they were paid by the Department of Education and Training."

Again we did not consider the gravity of the issue because both Ammih-jan and the general were now in the parliamentary prison and were allowed to attend Hammam-i-Golestan (a public bath) on the next day.

I heard that, following my grandmother's death, one of our brave relatives had visited them in the prison under the pretense of being the general's sister and having brought black clothes for them. (At the time I wrote this article, my mother was still alive. Now I can say that the brave relative was my mother.) I heard they had been reunited in one room several times. They had separate rooms. But later in Evin (prison), where the cell accommodated several others, the meetings were behind glass and through handsets.

Nevertheless, I figured that, since Ammih-jan was used to visiting prisons as a social worker in her youth, the environment was probably not so strange to her. She had stated in her will that she wanted to donate her clothes and chador to the female prison guard. In prison, a reporter from *Kayhan International* paid her a visit and conducted an interview, which was later published.

What do you think Grandmother meant? Which tradition should I continue?

I knew that both of them had suffered persecution in fighting for women's rights. But I did not know enough at the time. I was aware that my grandmother and grandfather (Farrokh-Din Parsay) published the *Jahan-i Zanan* magazine. Because of their association with this magazine, they were threatened and, finally, exiled. It was there that Ammih-jan was born. At the time of exile on their way to Qum, my grandmother was expecting Farrokh-Ru. Their crime was providing information to women and solving their day-to-day issues through the publication based in Mashhad.

Suddenly I remembered a little diary Ammih-jan gave me before her arrest and asked me to hide on her behalf. I took it out and read two to three pages and memorized its content. Then I contacted a friend who had a private business and

---

[11] An influential figure at the time who now headed the Ministry for Education and Training. He went on to become the prime minister for a short time.

asked if I could photocopy the diary. He allowed me to photocopy the diary in his office. I completed the photocopy over two days and hid it under my carpet at home. I heard that there are several other diaries that have either been sent abroad or kept with relatives. Fortunately the first volume of her diary relating to mother (Fakhr-Afaq Parsay) and her life was now with me.

Without the right to have a defense attorney, her defense statements in the ridiculous court were printed in the papers. She kept her promise, did not stay quiet for fear of losing her life, and spoke out against Beheshti and Bahonar. In her will, she advised everyone not to mourn her death. She asked her children to imagine she was killed in a plane crash. She wrote that she did not owe money to anyone.

In her final night's visit, she told her son and husband, "I have achieved my goals in life and succeeded in fighting for women's rights to the best of my ability. It is an honor not dying in a hospital bed."

Her son asked why she was talking like this.

She replied, "The gentlemen are planning for my execution."

Her son and husband pleaded. "But we have been promised a pardon from Bani Sadr."[12]

She simply answered, "As I said, the children are now grown and matured. I am now considered elderly (she was fifty-nine). Give my watch and ring to Mahshid."

Later Mahshid advised that once Ammih-jan requested a watch from her as she wanted to say prayers in prison and did not know the time. She always wanted my Baha'i ex-husband (son of General Sani'ee) and I to reconcile.

I wanted to tell her it was me who had married a Baha'i. Why did they accuse you? It was me who sang and danced. Why did they accuse you of prostitution?

I recall once at a restaurant at the wedding reception of her daughter Nahid, the band was playing. I knew she had a good voice and danced well during her youth and asked her to dance. She said, "It is not appropriate. People will talk. And besides, the general does not dance!"

Little did I know that, in fighting for women's rights, even at that stage, she had to tolerate so much hardship.

---

12 Abol-Hasan Bani Sadr was the elected President at this time.

It appears that both Beheshti and Bahonar wanted her silence. Khomeini was a known critic of women's rights. Years before he had issued a fatwa from Najaf against the liberation of women after a woman was appointed to a ministerial position.

Jahan-i Zanan (*Women's World*) magazine was initially published in Mashhad and later in Tehran. It was established in Mashhad under the name of F.A.P (Fakhr-Afaq Parasai) as the editor in chief. The first issue was dated February 4, 1921.

Every months, two issues were printed, and the contents as indicated on the front cover were "solely dedicated to the lives of women and importance of their education." Some of the titles in the first issue were:

"Action and Aspirations of Women around the World"

"Necessity of Training Women"

"Raising a Child"

"Famous Women"

"Cooking"

"Poems"

"Information"

Here is an extract from "Actions and Aspirations" in the first issue:

> Our virtues are chastity of the pen, tongue and body. Our aspirations are self education, belief in our superior station, necessity to follow religious obligations, living in harmony with our guardian/husband as to provide us with the basic material necessities and not be condemned to death under the severity of beatings, torture, or hanging by rope.
>
> We have elected to write at a time where the peoples of the earth have come to appreciate the station of woman and made her a real partner in their private lives. Women are asked to administer social affairs and have political and economic rights in accordance with the law of creation.
>
> However in our country we feel that, in complying to Islamic laws and regulations, when it comes to the education and training of

women, popular opposition prevents us from writing openly and leaves us only to highlight and convey the basic importance of the issue.

In particular soon after the conception of this magazine, the environment was contaminated by such jealousy and hatred that very nearly resulted in this infant becoming aborted, leaving the mother to mourn the death of the unborn child.

Now we have the honour to courageously put forward our considered views and reflections .. we do not wish to repeat the obvious. We reiterate that our aspirations and actions are based on the Islamic religion and regulations.

Farrokh Din Parsay, a veteran Iranian journalist, once described his early days in these words:

I married Fakhr-Afaq in 1913. This was at a time when Malak u'lshoara Bahar[13] had just arrived in Tehran. At this time, we had two children. As the income from the newly established *Akhlaq* newspaper was insufficient to cover the production costs, I took up a paid position with a newspaper in Mashhad in 1916 solely to support my family. I wrote articles for the *Chaman* newspaper, was the resident correspondent for the *Ra'd* newspaper and established the *Jahan-i Zanan* magazine managed by my wife.

In 1920 I accompanied the Afghan Ambassador to Tehran as the deputy host for his visit. I returned to Mashhad in two months. In 1921 I was appointed by Sayyid Zia'u'Din[14] the Chief Minister to manage the publications for the Ministry of Interior in Tehran. I came to Tehran for this purpose but the assignment was foiled after a month when Sayyid Zia'u'Din tendered his resignation.

The fifth edition of *Jahan-i Zanan* was published in Tehran in 1921. This issue indicated Farrokh-Din Parsay as the owner and Fakhr-Afaq Parsay as the editor in

[13] Bahar is a well known Iranian poet, author, and literary figure, with many books and articles to his name.
[14] Chief Minister prior to Reza Shah Pahlavi.

chief. The publication of this magazine in Tehran caused a stir, and many called on the owner, publisher, and editor to suffer religious sanctions. Here is how Farrokh-Din Parsay described the events:

> Upon returning [from Mashhad] and acting on my wife's insistence who had promised to publish *Jahan-i Zanan* in Tehran, the first edition of the publication was printed in this city. This coincided with the general opposition to the cabinet of Qavam u'l Saltanah.[15] His opponents used the contents of this magazine, essentially about the education and training of women, to mobilise the merchants [bazaar] against the Cabinet. Eventually the Chief Minister gave in to the opposition and arranged for the banishment of my family and I from Tehran in order to appease the Bazar. We were banished to Ara'k. On our arrival at Qum, we heard whispers of Takfir against myself and my wife apparently in progress at various gatherings in Tehran. I even witnessed a protest rally in a cemetery in Qum who called the female editor of *Jahan-i Zanan* magazine as an enemy of the Prophet. Around the same time a number of individuals were arrested in Ara'k for allegedly being a Baha'i and having burnt the Quran. For these reasons we refrained from going to Ara'k and settled in Qum. Later I returned to the public service as a Roads Inspector for the Tehran-Ara'k highway.

After much despair for not being pardoned by the authorities, the editor of *Jahan-i Zanan* prepared a statement addressed to the "Subscribers of *Jahan-i Zanan*" and published in the Iran newspaper dated December 1922:

Dear Subscribers:

In the end we were not taught freedom and eventually the freedom to write, publish and criticise was also taken away from the men. However

---

[15] A professional politician who assumed the position of prime minister several times during the Pahlavi reign.

I await that day, because quietism is a sign of little intellect. I may now pass away in waiting carrying the financial debt of subscribers with me. For this reason and having lost faith in restarting the publication, I wish to repay my debt at a time when the Magazine has suffered a loss of over 500 Toomans.

I do not have the documents relating to *Jahan-i Zanan* and have no means of identifying my out of pocket subscribers. Even if they are identified, forwarding small amounts ranging from 8 to 16 Qerans will encounter numerous difficulties. Therefore I request the loyal subscribers to send me their subscription receipts to the committee's address in Qom and indicate which editions they like to read. I can repay my debt through sending their requested editions and thereby say farewell to those loyal friends. After that I will wait for an effective general revolution which may even take me as a victim

Fakhr-Afaq Parsay

Jahan-i Zanan was never published again. Fakhr-Afaq was the first woman to have her publication stopped. Here is how her husband describes this intellectual lady:

My wife has a life unlike other ladies. Her education took her through upper school. From the start of our marriage she longed for freedom and reform. She regarded the Veil as a barrier to the progress of society. She was particularly skilled in educating her children and managed to raise our five children with distinction even though we were always on the road.

Farrokh-Ru Parsay

Farrokh-Ru was born on March 21, 1922, in exile at Qum. She would always start her autobiography with the name of her mother. Life was particularly difficult and unbearable for a mother who became pregnant in exile. Everyone knew why Fakhr-Afaq Parsay was banished to Qum.

Publication of her two articles in *Jahan-i Zanan* had caused a revolt. In these articles, she'd advocated for equal education and training for boys and girls. The mullahs quickly denounced her by using Takfir. One day Qavam u'l Saltanah, the then prime minister, summoned her husband, Farrokh-Din, and advised him to, "Take your wife and go to a remote location."

They rented a place outside of Qum. The family lived on a 200-tooman pension paid by the government. On the first day of Nawruz 1921, when the new year had barely began, Farrokh-Ru came in to this world. She was the second daughter born to the exiled mother. Farrokh-Zaman, her eldest, was eight years old at the time and later died at eighteen.

Their children were Farvardin, Farrokh-Zad, Farrokh Zaman, Farrokh-Ru, and Farrokh-pour. They longed for their daughters to become educated. In reality, they were unable to find a school in Qum even for their boys. Farrokh-Ru was barely one when they returned to Tehran. Her first day at school was in 1927 in a school known as "Sharq." Farrokh-Ru was in sixth grade when her father was asked by the Department of Roads to serve in Mashhad. She completed her middle school in the "Foruq" school in Mashhad. There the girls wore the chador to school, something Farrokh-Ru was careful to avoid. They returned to Tehran after three years.

Farrokh-Ru was one of the early graduates attending the Teacher Training College. She continued her postgraduate studies t the same college. In 1942, she was employed as a high school teacher at Noorbakhsh High School. She taught biology to the students in year seven. In 1944, she married a young army officer. His sister had, four years earlier, married her elder brother. The families had been close neighbors for close to fifteen years. Soon after their marriage, Officer Shirin Sokhan was appointed as the chief of the Kazeroon Brigade[16] and immediately left for duty. The couple was separated for three years, during which Farrokh-Ru studied at the College of Medicine.

In 1948, at the time she was still a student, her first child was born. Hamid was

---

[16] A town in the southwestern province of Khuzestan.

only four months old when she became pregnant with Nahid. She had two infants at the time she did her thesis. In 1950, she became the biology teacher at Jandark High School, where she stayed on until 1956. This is how she recalls the events:

> When I wanted to become the School Principal, I said to my husband: I will not be in the house for many hours in a day. Do you approve? He accepted and advised: I am confident that you are aware of your responsibilities in the home just as you manage your responsibilities outside of the home.

After completion of her daily work in the high school, she would visit women prisoners in various jails and educate them in her capacity as a social worker.

At this time, she gave birth to two other daughters, Mahshid and Navid.

For one year, she was the principal of Valli u'llah Nasr High School. In 1957, she was appointed to head Noorbaksh High School, whose name was later changed to Reza Shah Kabir. At that time, the school had about 110 female students. When Farrokh-Ru retired from education and joined the Majlis, she said farewell to 1,850 female students. Here is how she described it:

> Heading an all girls' school is more onerous than being a Minister! Sometimes a School Principal is confronted with specific problems whose solution requires the intellect of ten Ministers. For example from my 1,000 female students in the high school, perhaps 70–80 displayed abnormal behaviours. At the time I was trying to figure out the reasons for this. I made up questionnaires and ordered the teachers to complete them during the course of the year. In these questionnaires the teachers were asked to document the mental state of each girl. I witnessed how family problems resulted in the discontent and rebellion amongst the girls. It was common for people to view Noorbaksh High School as a school for the wealthy and the well off. Reality struck me at once when I observed that one of my students is becoming weaker day by day. One day close to lunch time she fainted.

I discovered that she had not eaten well for three days, her parents had divorced years ago, her mother supported the family with a daily 3 Tooman income from sewing but had elected to send her daughter to the best school in Tehran.[17]

Farrokh-Ru joined the Mehregan Club, which was a de facto union for the teachers soon after its establishment in 1951. Just like her mother, she wanted to assist in building a better life for women and achieving equality with men. She desired for all women to further their place in society and use their expertise in all areas. She was a feminist dedicated to achieving equality for women through the political system. For this reason, prior to the infamous referendum in February 1962, she would organize rallies for women, to campaign for their right to vote. In April 1962, she joined Kanun-i Tarraqi (Association for Progress) established by Hasan Ali Mansour. When this association became a political party, she became one of its first female delegates to the 21st Majlis. She was appointed to the Parliamentary Committees for Budget, Culture and Family. She campaigned for reforms to the laws governing family life that led to the passing of the "Family Support" bill.

Following the murder of Hasan Ali Mansour, she was appointed as the Minister for Education and Training by the new Prime Minister Amir Abbas Hoveyda, thereby becoming the first woman to become a Minister in Iran.

As a minister, she appointed educated women to positions previously occupied by men. She was instrumental in establishing the cultural center of southern Tehran with more than 5,000 male and female students under the management of Ms. Najmi Vusuqi. Her other priority was the distribution of free food[18] in state schools that, in practice, encountered real obstacles by way of corruption, lack of an effective distribution system and little coordination between various government departments.

---

[17] Interview with M. Peernia printed in *Zan-i Ruz* magazine, 1976.

[18] Known as "Taqzieh Rayegan" or free nourishment.

Farrokh-Ru assisted in writing a book entitled *Woman in Ancient Iran* with Homa Ahi and Malakeh Taliqani.

She was convicted to death without due process in a courtroom in April 1980. Just before her execution, they wrapped her in a thick bag and then sprayed her with bullets.

CHAPTER 45

MONTEREY, 2006

As I moved from Lompoc to Monterey, I first found an apartment close to the base. I could walk to the gate and could see the ocean from my window. The landlord said, "All new teachers of DLI enter my apartment happy and gradually become very sad and angry. I don't know why."

The pressure is too great, and you are among military while you are a civilian. You have to obey too many rules. But I loved my students. I still am friends with some, and just yesterday, a student found me on Facebook and asked me to translate a sentence for him so he could tattoo it in Farsi on his back. I don't like tattoos, but I did what he asked me and wrote the sentence and sent the picture to him.

Of all my students, I liked a girl called Arezoo and a boy called Parham or Peyvand (his real name started with K). As soon as the soldiers would start the school, we would give them a Persian name. That was why I remember most of them by their Farsi name. I heard so many stories from them. One's father raped her for years. Another, in Puerto Rico, saw many guns and drugs from the gangs. They would talk, practicing the language, and I loved them all.

But the staff side and the rules applied to us were very difficult. All doctors in town were treating the teachers of DLI and knew it. Sometimes our old students were killed in the war, and we'd spent the whole year in a room with them and would get so sad. Some would return from the war and not enough care or psychiatric care was given to them. The Iraq War really affected them, especially when no weapons of mass destructions were found. I remembered the brother of Becky, my old roommate. Since the Vietnam War until now, not much was done for the soldiers when they returned from wars to give them free treatments psychologically. That is another burden on my heart.

I am glad I left that town, although it was very rich in culture and I learned a lot on language day, when all cultures were celebrated from all over the world. I miss my students and wish them all well.

Telling it all about the rape in Monterey, 2006

In psychological terms, at one point, you have to throw up what's been in your throat for a long time. I was at the end of pretending as if it wasn't important that my sister's husband took advantage of me that I had to constantly dodge his flirting comments.

Since that day in Berlin, he dropped comments in my email inbox and on my phones, saying basically, "Please, let me love you." After thirty years, when I had my shoulder surgery in 2006 in Castroville, California, my sister and her second daughter Yasi, came to take care of me. I was taking heavy-duty pain killers, and after couple of days, I could not take it any longer . Sometimes you have to vomit what you have kept inside for a long, long time. I said, "Your husband took advantage of me. Leave me alone and stop pretending as if you love me and have come to take care of me."

She quickly summoned her daughter, and they left in a taxi to San Jose, heading back to Texas where my sister, her husband, and her eldest daughter live.

Since the day that I decided to tell all about exactly what happened, all of the relatives took the man's side. One even said, "It takes two to tango!"

With one sentence, the ignorant justifies all the rapes in the world. Even for married couples, if the woman is in a situation in which she has to submit and doesn't really want to engage in sexual intercourse, the word is *rape.*

The worst retribution for my truth telling came was when all my relatives stopped inviting me to their houses for any occasion. The once-a-year gathering during which I could see my son, which was very important to me, was stopped. Why? Because after thirty years, I told the total truth. Before I had not dared to say the whole truth and would just hint to everybody that, if there was a remote possibility that guy would be there, I would not attend that family gathering. And all thought it was because of his infidelity during the affair with the German woman's when he left my sister for a while. Only my sister and mother knew most of the story, and both decided to deny it and keep the honor.

I don't think my sister is part of the women's lib struggle, as she obviously looked the other way and blamed me and not her husband. She did not ask why he returned to Iran so quickly after I went to Germany. We heard that the German woman gave birth to a son. That was why my sister got pregnant again, hoping she had a son, but she had a beautiful girl with green eyes. But even when they were in my house on last day I saw them fifteen years ago and asked her in front of her daughter, what is the color of Yasi's eyes, my sister said "blue," which is the color of her husband's eyes. That to me is like a frog that someone stepped on.

I am sure Sepideh, her eldest daughter, believes me because she was close to eight or so at that time and can remember everything discussed at that dinner table. Once I asked Mehrdad, "Why did you do that? What gave you the permission to tell me you loved me and do that?"

He said, "Well when you got off the plane and looked at me, you got all red, and I figured you liked me."

If you understand that answer, please explain it to me. Does that means, if a girl gets angry with you and gets red, it's a welcome sign? Only opportunists would interpret it that way.

As I was writing this book I found out that all these years my sister never confronted her husband. Never. Shame.

CHAPTER 46

OTHER EVENTS IN MONTEREY, 2007–2017

As I said, again I collected all my furniture and moved to Monterey as the government gave me a job as a Farsi teacher at the Defense Language Institute (DLI). I became a federal employee. I loved my job but did not like the fact that I was treated like military personnel, when it came to the rules, and I was a citizen. Some rules were not easy. In addition, my coworkers made it feel like we were working in Iran, and jealousy and who knows who was in effect.

I first rented a house in Monterey itself. Then I bought a house in a park in Castroville, a huge manufactured house. Later, I bought a beautiful house on top of the hills on Soledad Drive in Monterey. I was fifteen minutes from Carmel, a city my mother had always loved. But she was not around anymore to enjoy it.

One of my neighbors in the Castroville manufactured house was a French Jewish woman called Yvonne. She was married to this Irish Catholic man. Both were around eighty-five at that time. She had a heavy French accent. Once she told me about her memories during the war, and I recorded the conversation. She said her brother was captured and was in a concentration camp. When he was released from the camp, he was very thin and had lice. She said they had a bakery, and she was a great cook. Being French and a great cook was a blessing for her husband. She decorated my house, and it came out beautifully. She and Ray, a ninety-two year old man who I met in that park, were enjoying moving my stuff around. To thank them, I took them to a Persian restaurant. They both slept on the way to and from the restaurant!

I heard that Marilyn Monroe was the artichoke queen of that town once. I also once saw Yvonne giving commune in a church in Castroville to the people. Go figure! I had lots of great artichokes there, fried and boiled.

In addition, I have good memories adopting two little girls called Melissa and Jewel through a program of friendship. The two girls lived in Castroville. Melissa was my Avon lady's, daughter. And Jewel was a beautiful little Jewish girl who had lost her own father. I found her through a Boys and Girls Club program. Those were happy days of my life.

My son's girlfriend's sister, Crystal, a veterinarian, lived in Monterey too, and that gave me an opportunity to see my son. He and Claudia would visit her or me on their way to San Francisco to visit Claudia's parents.

While living there, I bought another Toyota Camry, just like the one my last husband had stolen from me. I did it just to make a statement to my ex that, whether he knew it or not, I was as good without him. I also got my second master's degree from the Chapman University in education, another statement to my ex—I could get a degree without him helping me. I was still under the influence of that nasty divorce, and I hated men and the idea of any relationship.

Strange neighbor in Monterey, 2008

When you first enter a country, for years and years, you think all the people are so nice because you don't understand the language and the laws well enough to see and understand the bad side of people too. You don't get half the jokes or sarcastic comments. To me, all was fine until I got this neighbor in the best part of Monterey. When I bought my beautiful house, I got a neighbor to the left. The guy and his wife lived downstairs. Their daughter, along with two dogs and three cats, lived upstairs. I befriended them as my neighbors.

One day, my neighbor started building a greenhouse at the border of my house and theirs. I saw him come into my side to extend it. One day when I came home, I saw him with a spade on my side of the border, digging something. Even the police were furious, and this was the second time that the police had taken my side. I called the police. The police made a report and suggested I get my house borders measured by a land surveyor. I had to pay close to $2,000 dollars to do that. In the end, the court granted me exactly how much I'd paid for the measurement and lawyers' fees. My time and effort did not add up, but they had to destroy that green house and retreat much farther back. They were way into my side of the house. They were trespassing.

Also, when rain came, all the water flowed to my house due to their wrong planning. I called the police again and mentioned it, but they refused to listen. So I had to go to court. The first time, the trick was that the judge was not there, so our hearing was cancelled. So I got a lawyer, and we went to court again. This time, they were charged with trespassing.

What they did next was what made even the police angry. They had to compensate me for the money I'd spent, close to $3,000. They filled two buckets full of coins adding up to $3,000 and left the two heavy buckets in front of my house down the hill. I had to call the police again, and they put the buckets in my trunk and asked me to park my car back up the hill with the back of the car to the garage door so my neighbors would not come and take them from my car. The police usually know better.

The next day, I drove to my bank, which had a penny counter machine, and deposited the money into my account.

Those neighbors were also very stingy, and I regret inviting them to my house for Thanksgiving the year before. And after that incident, I cut all connections with them. My neighbor to the right died, and her house was sold to a nice couple with a dog called Mojo. Those neighbors were nice. I would give an apple every so often to Mojo, and they called me the apple lady. The husband helped me a lot, and God gave me a nice neighbor. I am being nice here not mentioning their real names.

After I retired, I sold that house and got ready to move closer to my son, thought not in the same town. That was my son's wish, and I granted it, although deep in my heart, I hoped to live on the same block with him. I wanted to help him raise his kids and get a chance to be with his kids and him and make up for all the years of separation.

CHAPTER 47

BABAK'S WEDDING, 2008

In December 2008, my son sent an invitation to his wedding. He and Claudia were getting married in San Francisco. The ceremony was in three days and at different restaurants—there were New Zealand, Italian, Korean, and Chinese restaurants but no Persian restaurant. The marriage was done in San Francisco's city hall. Bahman and his third wife, Terry, and his third son, Chris, were there, along with Claudia's parents and sister and brother and a couple of their friends. We visited a museum before the ceremony, and Claudia made sure I understood that China was much larger than Iran. Later at the Korean restaurant, Bijan, Bahman's brother, walked in, and I hugged him. During the wedding, I called Touri Joon, Babak's paternal grandma, and thanked her for taking care of Babak. I thought I owed her that. Terry said, "Oh, she talks to you? I am not welcome in her house."

I was excited because I could have a grandchild soon. At last, my son was married and had his own family. I also thanked my car's navigator because we had to go to all of the different restaurants in different parts of San Francisco.

At the Chinese restaurant on the second day, Claudia wore red, as Chinese do. Her sweet grandpa was there too. I had the best Chinese food there, and all other Chinese food we have in different cities of America is just an imitation. You should go with someone who is Chinese and let him or her order—something Claudia refused to do the first day Babak and I and Claudia went to this restaurant in Virginia called Sunflower, just because they had vegetarian food and came out to be a Chinese restaurant.

At any rate, our destiny weaved us with the Chinese, and that was a big change .

I found out how racist I was but also how different we are at some points. I gave Claudia a beautiful turquoise and gold necklace that I have never seen her wearing—pity. I stopped giving her real jewelry except the ring of my mother, which was a diamond and sapphire. I hope she passes it to their daughter at her wedding.

Later they moved to Pasadena. She worked for Pixar and then Disney. She does not accept my friendship on Facebook. And so far, while their first son is seven, she never called me to say happy anything and has never given me her cell. She barely points her head at the camera and says hello and leaves during FaceTime calls. When they come over, she says and laughs the minimum. My patience is running out. But now, they are the young and the restless. I hope she does not judge me without knowing the whole truth. And for that matter, I hope my son finds it in his heart to forgive me. I know that today, as I am writing this and it's my son's birthday, I am crying. I am not okay with the mistreatment; my system is rejecting any disrespect or indifference from them.

Babak and Claudia had their first son, Elias, in 2013 and then their second son Alexander after a year and, later, a daughter called Kara. I'll never forget holding my first grandchild in my arms—a mixture of feelings of happiness and worry filled me. Should I love him? Would he be taken away from me like my son after I fell in love with him? Could I experience all childhood events that I never witnessed with my son through this child? I am in love with him and all the kids. But my heart used to long for one person, my son. Now I long for four people, my son and grandkids. I like Claudia, but it seems like she doesn't want to have anything to do with me, though I never disagreed with their marriage or anything. I don't see my grandkids on their birthdays. Twice a year is the most I get. I am only an hour away from them. I send ten messages to get one back, and I'd like to get my respect back, so maybe I'll stop. Is it my destiny or karma and I should accept it? As difficult as it is sometimes.

After living for eight years in Monterey, I sold my two houses in 2016, a condo that I'd bought with my mother's inheritance money and my own house that I lived in. I bought a house in a fifty-five-plus community in Camarillo and live in a two-bedroom, two-bath house. I thank God for that every day. I ask my son and his kids every year to come and visit and use the huge pool that I have and am told by my son that I should not show the pool to his kids, since they will be asking to come over! It's another knife in my heart. I am retired now, but maybe next year I will find a part-time job after I finish this book. Now I am here, an hour away from my son and his family. But I see them two to three times a year for an hour.

CHAPTER 48

SELF-RESPECT AND HAPPINESS

Since I witnessed parts of Iran's history, I felt I had to write about it. I'm also trying to answer some questions that my son or his children may have later.

I still am in a waiting status. I checked my weblog, and last time I saw Babak on his exact birthday was in 2005. After his second birthday and my divorce—the rest of my life—I was away from my son on all his special days, and he got used to seeing me a couple times a year. All his birthdays, New Years celebrations, Christmases, and Thanksgiving Days were missed. I could see him in the month of an event, and the same goes for my grandkids. So I call it birth month, not birthday, and I am lucky if it even happens then. I don't have my daughter-in-law's phone number or email, and she doesn't befriend me on Facebook. I never disagreed with this marriage and love them all, but something is not right here. I don't know what else I should do to be forgiven. I remain. Days of my life are rarely happy, and something at the corner of my heart is always longing, waiting, and hoping.

Once, when I went to my grandkid's soccer game, I wanted to scream and cry. I never went to my son's games. I shared it with him. It was painful for both I suppose. But my son never shows his real emotions, except some angers toward me. I also have not made a major mistake since I got closer to my son—no relationships and no wrong ones. No matter what, the most important thing for me is the relationship with my son and his family. I do self-therapies to learn how to be happy under any circumstances—easier said than done. But I like the focus of my life now on self-respect. All together, I have seen my son for 365 days, which is a year in this forty some years. I've learned to forgive all, but I can't forget.

I'd like to thank Mani and Afsaneh, who helped me at my hardest times. Unlike most of other relatives and siblings, they visited me during my nasty divorce in 2000. They also loaned me their car.

I'd like to thank Mali and Manigeh, my cousins, for always encouraging me. I thank God for having a beautiful home, being well educated, having had good jobs, and making enough money to run my life without getting help from anybody. Mali once told me, "*Love yourself. Respect* yourself."

And God knows I am trying. As I forgive whoever did me wrong, I can't help but to expect apologies deep in my heart. I pray for a better relationship with my son and family. I meant well. I also need to forgive myself.

Happiness

Now when I think back, I ask myself, Where and when was I happy? I see that, of course, every time I see my son, putting the humiliation I feel aside, I am happy. Then there are my trips to Cancun. I felt peaceful there. I have good memories of the early days of my first marriage. We were happy too.

Another time of happiness was when, during my childhood, the whole family would go to this city called Damavand, which has the largest mountain in Iran. The whole family and relatives would rent houses with fruit gardens.

Then happiness was at the camping at the Caspian seaside—all fun and happiness with people my age. I made good friends. I had good high school friends. Babak's birth was a happy occasion. He is my one and only child. I was also happy when I was writing my first book, *Women and Rules of the Society*, and when I was publishing my magazine for women, *Jahan Zanan dar Asre Aahan*. The name is a mix of my grandma's and my grandpa's newspapers. I combined them for the title of the little monthly paper I was publishing by myself. Also I feel happy and in harmony when I am making ceramics and/or art of any kind and when I am meditating. I felt good too, when I was calling this guy called Mr. Meybodi for the purpose of giving information to people over the radio—being useful and caring. I also enjoy my time when I am reading. Eating the food of Maman Zinat Joon, my grandma, was always pleasurable. Breastfeeding my baby, Babak, was a happy time. And his graduation from Cornell and UC Davis were very nice and happy times. Knowing my son has a good mind and is smart (I don't understand one word of the articles he writes on chemistry, math, physics, or computer) makes me happy. Watching him being such a good father is a joy. These are the pleasurable times of my life.

I need to ask my son for forgiveness for being young and restless, making wrong decisions, and not believing that the most important thing in life was him and him alone. I want to tell him, "Stop being angry at yourself. Don't look at yourself as a victim. Forgive your inexperienced parents and move on. It's good for your kids to have their real grandma around them and genes stay together. We only have that now. Let's embrace it."

CHAPTER 49

A LETTER TO MY SON

Stress is caused by being here but wanting to be there.

—Elkhart Tolle

Just as I lived all my life with the telephone and pictures as the closest thing to having my son, I also did not see the graves of my grandma, Maman Zinat Joon, or of my mother or my uncle, daee Farhang, or my cousin Hamid. Some I have seen only in pictures and some not at all. I keep asking the little family I have left in Iran who I am in contact with to send me those pictures. But they have their own problems living under the brutal, unusual, and falsely religious regime of Iran. I understand. But now at this corona time, where no one can see their children or grandchildren for a very short time, they may understand what I have gone through all my life. I still live for pictures as my best memories.

My therapist asked me to write a letter to my son. Here it is:

> I am in therapy now. My therapist has said that I need to tell you the truth of my situation. I was never strong enough to do that . My only goal is to give you the facts in the hope that the past can be made peace with, so that we can have a loving and happy future.
>
> One day, if you want to hear everything from my view, I would love to tell you. Please understand that, while I take full responsibility for myself, there are two sides to every story—the story that you have been told and believe and the story that I actually lived. Somewhere in the middle is the truth.

Regardless, I want to apologize for not being the mother you needed and wanted, for not being available in your life, and for any way that I caused you any kind of hurt or sorrow. We can't change the past, but we can certainly create a more loving and happy relationship in the future. I will do anything in my power for this to happen, I just ask that you all let me know what you need and what you want, and I will do my best . I am willing to go to therapy with you, whatever it takes. Please just let me know.

Love,
Roya

The power of a son is way, way stronger than anything. Seeing him cures you; not seeing him breaks you.

CHAPTER 50

QUOTATIONS

Living is a form of not being sure, not knowing what next or how. The moment
you know how, you begin to die a little. The artist never entirely knows.
We guess. We may be wrong, but we take leap after leap in the dark.

—Agnes de Mille

I can only add that if you want to read more about my life, you can search Google
for my name, Roya Parsay, and get to my blog called *My Unedited Life*.

There is a book about Dr. Parsay, my aunt, called *Lady Minister* (*Khanum Vazir*
in Farsi). I'll translate just one page of the book by Mrs. Pirnia (page 272):

Queen Farah Pahlavi said, "After we heard the news of the execution
of Dr. Farrokh Rou Parsay, the king and I were so sad. After the Shah
heard the news in exile, he went sadly into his room and did not return
for hours. No one dared to go talk to him and ask any questions.
Queen Farah herself was a student of my aunt in Jeanne d'Arc School.
The queen, at the twentieth anniversary of Dr. Parsay's death, said in
a message, "The history of Iran will remember Farrokh Rou Parsay as
a hero who, until the last moment of her life, was fighting for women's
liberation." Mrs. Parsay, in the prison, said, "I welcome death and am
not willing to accept the mandatory hijab just to live days longer."
(Remember that she and her mother put all their efforts in life into
freeing women from the hijab.) The queen said, "This is what my
teacher [Dr. Parsay] said."

Also Prince Reza Pahlavi said, "The history of women's struggle for equality was done by some determined women. We hope the name and memory of Dr. Farrokh Rou Parsay, this capable citizen of Iran, is always mentioned parallel to glory. The new generation shall not forget her. Her way of freeing women from prejudice and captivity is continued further and more."

The twin sister of the king, Princess Ashraf [the one in the photograph with my grandma and other pioneer women that was the only picture in my grandma's room], in a letter to all famous newspapers of the world, condemned "the unjust, short trial and sentence of Dr. Parsay without having a lawyer."

Women of the world should have united. The UN and Amnesty International should have pursued it. Human rights are not practiced in Iran. But for this woman, my aunt, the world did not do what was right and just. I still expect more.

Last Notes and Dates

Choosing the pictures in this book was very difficult. Since I live with the pictures replacing physically seeing and meeting my son, I have more than a normal person's number of pictures. So it was too difficult to choose them. Also my son will not let me put pictures of my grandkids on Facebook or include them in this book at all. He made that quite clear. If he had a choice he would even like for me to omit his pictures too. He told me that last week and broke my heart again. But I am playing "deaf and blind and dumb" again, per the advice of a psychologist. I have to get permission for everything—what I say and do—so I won't lose my privilege of seeing my son and my grandkids and his immediate family.

Babak worked for Pixar and helped making *Finding Nemo*, and Claudia worked on more movies, especially *Brave*. The red hair of the main character was designed by Claudia. I am proud of both of them.

When *Finding Nemo* was made, I was between jobs and working at a bank in

Virginia at the window section of the bank. I told almost everyone who came to the bank to go see the movie *Finding Nemo* and, way in the end of it, they would see the name of my son, Babak Sanii, and my daughter-in-law, Claudia Chung Sanii.

Babak's Pixar business card says "Laser Dude" as his job title. I love this place, now bought by Disney. I visited once, greeted by the statue of a blue monster at the door. There was a volleyball playground, a statue building room, and lots of activities you don't normally see in any office. But features were cleverly sharpening the creativity of all who worked there. You get the best out of your employees that way.

Now Babak has left Pixar. He works as a professor at a college and does amazing stuff that, even when I read his reports, I don't understand a word. He is a genius all right.

I am hoping that, one day, my son will shout, "I am tired of being angry"—as Nema, a character in the *Shahs of Sunset* on TV did last night. Nema's parents got separated when he was very young, and he lived with his father while his sister lived with his mother. He had to go through double separation. He never forgave his parents and as always angry around them until he got fed up with his anger.

I have also told my story on YouTube but in Farsi. A simple search for Roya Parsay takes you to different places. But I will make more audio and video clips and add them to YouTube in the future or put them on Amazon.

As I was finishing this book, my son informed me that him and his wife and my grand children are all moving to San Francisco, about eight hours away from me. So my short lived happiness of being close to him and the kids was over. Also with the help of some of my women friends, we helped a boy in Iran to have a successful brain surgery.

I am planning to stay alive to see my grandchildren's weddings. Life continues to change every minute some sweet and some bitter, but I try to live the rest of my life as mindful as I can. It's inevitable that all lives are a bowl of changes, but I hope my life as a bowl of changes will, now and then, be mixed with a bowl of sweet cherries.

CHRONOLOGY OF EVENTS

1952. I was born in November in the south of Iran near the Persian Gulf. Months before that date, Father composed a poem about Mosaddegh in the oil company in Abadan near the Persian Gulf, sent to me by Dr. Matin Daftari, Mosaddegh's grandson.

1953. Had my first operation at six months old (intestinal twist).

1954. Mosaddegh was toppled. My brother Farzad (Mosaddegh) was born.

1962. Had my second operation (hernia, repair of first operation, and appendix) while living at my paternal grandma's house.

1967. Maternal grandpa, Mehdi Massihnia, dies of heart problem. I was fifteen.

1968. Met the Shah and Queen Farah as a flower girl on several occasions.

1969. Went to America, Earlham College Richmond, Indiana.

1970. Returned to Tehran, Iran, during Earlham summer vacation.

1971. Went to Purdue University, got a scholarship.

1971. Paternal grandpa, Farrokh Din Parsay, died.

1973. Married Bahman Sanii in Iran.

1973. Returned to America, Purdue University, Indiana. Later Bahman joined me.

1974. Graduated in computer sciences from Purdue University, Indiana.

1974–75. Returned to Tehran via England, Switzerland, and Austria.

1977. Babak, my only son with Bahman, was born in Tehran in March.

1979. Mohammad Reza Shah and Queen Farah Pahlavi of Iran left the country.

1979. Revolution in Iran happened. Khomeini, a clergyman, entered Iran as its leader.

1979. Divorced Bahman, father of Babak, my only son.

1979. General Sanii, former secretary of defense and grandfather of my son was arrested and released after six months, bailed out by his brother.

1980. Dr. Farrokh Rou Parsay, my paternal aunt and former secretary of education, and her husband, General Shirin Sokhan, were arrested.

1980. Bahman and Babak left Iran, heading first to England and then Switzerland and, finally, Canada.

1980. Fakhr Afagh Parsay, my paternal grandmother, died of heartbreak seeing her daughter taken to prison by guards.

1980. General Sanii was threatened with arrest again per his book *Memories and Memoires*.

1980. Dr. Farrokh Rou Parsay, my aunt, was executed via firing squad by the regime of Iran.

1981. Went to Berlin, a trip arranged by my sister, to see her husband, Mehrdad. I was taken advantage of by him there.

1981. Left Iran for Switzerland to see my son, Babak.

1981. Saw Babak after a year of separation.

1983. Bahman and Babak left Switzerland for Canada.

1983. Returned to Iran for my first trip back after the revolution and married Farrokh to rescue him from the Iran-Iraq War.

1984. Divorced Farrokh after six months. He went to the United States, as was his plan.

1985. Returned to the United States to my brother Farzad's house from Geneva.

1986. Moved to my own condo in Falls Church, a block away from my brother.

1986. Got my green card through my computer job.

1990. Got my US citizenship.

1991. Father died of a stroke after being in a coma for months. My sister hid it from me.

1992. Went to Iran for the last time to spend time with my grandma and see my father's grave.

1992. Visited the Caspian Sea, Ramsar, and Hamadan in Iran with the mandatory hijab,

1992. Returned to the United States from Tehran for the last time.

1992. Three months later, my maternal grandma, Zinat Sadat Yamotahari, died. I never saw her grave.

1993. Mother's first cancer operation (breast cancer) in Reston, Virginia.

1993. Rented a house in Falls Church so Mother could live with me.

1994. Went to Paris with my brother Farhad to an NCR meeting.

1996–97. Published my newspaper called *Jahan Zanan dar Asr Ahan* (*World of Women in the Iron Era*), a combination of the names of the two newspapers my paternal grandparents had in the year 1920.

1997. General Asadollah Sanii, my son's grandpa and former secretary of defense died in Canada.

1998. Hamid Shirin Sokhan, my cousin, died of a heart attack at the age of forty-eight-ish.

1998. Started my own business of a Mediterranean store called Asia Market-Mehr.

1998. Took Mother to the social security office and started her health care paperwork.

1998. Rented an apartment in Alexandria for Mother above my own condo.

2000. Married Mehrdad in DC, an SEU professor, for a year.

2000. Mother's second operation for cancer of the bladder, which failed, in Virginia.

2001. Mother died of cancer in Iran, November, Thanksgiving Day.

2001. Got my MBA in information technology from SEU.

2002. Divorce process with Mehrdad started in Virginia.

2003. Finalized divorce from Mehrdad.

2003. Bought a condo in Reston, Virginia, and moved there.

2004. Left for California from Virginia driving a truck with Dick Holmberg, my coworker.

2006. Left Lompoc for Monterey to work at DLI teaching soldiers.

2006. Uncle Dr. Farhang Massihnia died of brain cancer in Iran.

2008. Bought a house in Monterey, California, near Carmel and a rental condo in Monterey, California.

2008. Babak married Claudia in San Francisco.

2010. Got a master's in education from Chapman University in Monterey, California.

2011. Uncle Houshang Massihnia died of cancer in California.

2013. First grandchild, Elias, was born.

2014. Second grandchild, Alexander, was born.

2016. Retired and sold houses in Monterey.

2017. Bought a house in Camarillo and moved there.

2018. Third grandchild, Kara, was born.

2020. Finished writing this book.

Printed in the United States
By Bookmasters